SCREW UNTO OTHERS

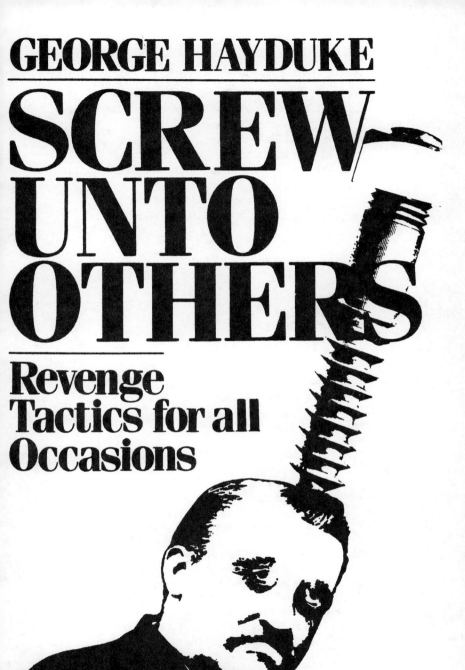

GEORGE HAYDUKE

SCREW UNTO OTHERS

Revenge Tactics for all Occasions

PALADIN PRESS
BOULDER, CO

Also by George Hayduke:

Get Even: The Complete Books of Dirty Tricks
Get Even 2: More Dirty Tricks from the Master of Revenge
The Hayduke Silencer Book
Make 'em Pay! Ultimate Revenge Techniques from
    the Master Trickster
Make My Day! Hayduke's Best Revenge Techniques for
    the Punks in Your Life
Silent But Deadly: More Homemade Silencers
Up Yours! Guide to Advanced Revenge Techniques

Screw Unto Others:
Revenge Tactics for All Occasions
by George Hayduke

Copyright © 1987 by George Hayduke

ISBN 0-87364-405-0
Printed in the United States of America

Published by Paladin Press, a division of
Paladin Enterprises, Inc.
Gunbarrel Tech Center
7077 Winchester Circle
Boulder, Colorado 80301 USA
+1.303.443.7250

Direct inquiries and/or orders to the above address.

Visit our Web site at www.paladin-press.com

Contents

Hello 1
Write to Me 4
How to Use This Wonderful Book 6
General Advice 7
The Eleven Commandments of Revenge 10
Caution 12
Additives 13
Airlines 14
Alarm Clocks 16
Animal Scent 18
Answering Machines 19
Apartments 20
Arrests 21
Attacks on Haydukery 22
Auto Dealers 23
Auto Keys 24
Automobiles 25
Awards 31
Banks 33
Billboards 35
Bitchy Calls 36
Body Fluids and Semifluids 37

Boomboxes 39
Bovine Effluvia 41
Bumper Stickers 43
Burials 44
Camp Counselors 45
Cassette Tapes 47
Castration 48
Cement 50
Chemicals 51
Coin-Operated Machines 54
College Bookstores 55
Computers . . . . , . . . 56
Condoms 58
Contests 60
Contra Aid 61
Controversy Clearing House 63
Corporate/Institutional 65
Creative Editing 67
Credit Cards 69
Cult Stuff 70
Customs 71
Dead Animals 72
Dogs 73
Doorknobs 74
Drugs 75
Ecotage 77
Excrement 79
Exotic Weapons 81
Explosives 82
Fart 83
Farting and Beyond 85
Food 86
Food Stamps 88
Furniture Stores 89
Garbage 90
Gasoline 91
Gelatin 93
Gossips 94

Graffiti 95
Gravesites 97
Guns 99
Hangovers 101
Help Lines 103
Highways 105
Hit 'n Run Drivers 106
Horns 107
Impersonations 108
Incinerators 109
Interoffice Memos 110
Intestines 111
IRS 112
Jocks 113
Junque Mail 114
Jury Duty 115
Landlords 116
Law Enforcement 117
Lawns 119
Leprosy 121
Letters 122
Machismo 123
Mafia 124
Mail 125
Mail Forwarding 127
Magazines 128
Meat Shoppes 130
Media 131
Medical 133
Mercenary 134
Military 135
Milk Carton Kids 138
Molesters 140
Motels 142
Neighbors 144
Newspapers 147
Obscene Telephone Calls 148
Packages 149

Paint 150
Pear Trees...................................151
Personal Products...........................152
Pets 153
Photofinishing 154
Pinball Machines............................156
Plants...157
Plastic Money................................158
Playing Cards................................159
Poison Ivy....................................160
Politicians 161
Pornography 163
Postal Stuff...................................165
Prey TV.......................................166
Pricks...168
Pubic Hair....................................170
Quotes 172
Religion 174
Restaurants...................................176
Rocketry......................................178
Satellite Television...........................179
Septic Tanks..................................180
Sex Toys......................................181
Shell Casings.................................183
Shoplifting 184
Smokers.......................................185
Sneezing and Coughing......................186
Sources 187
Spray Paint...................................196
Stencils 198
Strobes 'n Stereos............................199
Stupid "Success" Story.......................201
Stupid "Success" Story, Pt. II.................202
Subversives...................................204
Success Stories................................205
Super Glues...................................207
Supermarkets 208
Sweeties......................................210

Swimming Pools..............................213
Tampons.....................................215
Telephones..................................216
Toilets.....................................219
Toothpaste..................................220
Travel......................................221
Trees.......................................223
Turntables..................................224
Useful Addresses............................225
Vending Machines............................227
Windows.....................................228
Wrong Numbers...............................229
Zymurgy . . . The Last Word.................231

Kissing

A man may kiss his wife goodby,
The rose may kiss the butterfly,
The wine may kiss the frosted glass,
And you, my friend, may kiss my ass.

Hello . . .

Wonderful events can sprout when you plant the seeds of distrust in a garden of assholes. This, despite the critical view that revenge against bullies has lost its erection because we are pretty much an officially soft society. Back when Teddy Roosevelt, one of my all-time favorites, was president, a Moroccan sultan kidnapped an American citizen named Perdicaris. Not only did Teddy send a naval fleet to this one hostage's rescue, he also sent the orders: "Perdicaris alive and free or Raisuli (the sultan) dead and unburied." We no longer live in roughriding times, despite the mythical bullshit of Rambo and his PR man, Ronald Teflon Reagan. I mean, there are still MIAs and Khadaffi Duck still lives.

Happily for you and me, despite centuries of efforts by humanitarians to change our beliefs, the majority of people still cling to the primal urge to get even with someone who's done them a disfavor. All sorts of kindly folks have tried to wean us away from vengeance (e.g., governments seek to outlaw it) and, when that fails, attempt to channel vengeance into more acceptable forms of social expression, like war.

The truth is, in today's real world, hate, meanness,

1

and violence rarely take a nap. America's favorite "sport" is pro wrestling, while tough guy contests are making a comeback. Some women even say they are sick of sensitive men and that they just want to get laid. Aren't the robber barons back where they belong — busting unions and terrorizing the slave labor? Mean is as American as apple pie, and, with that, I apologize to Stokely Carmichael for updating his line from a generation or so ago.

When I was on a talk show panel in Chicago, another guest, a fuddy-duddy who was also a psychologist, told me that my revenge antics were anti-social. To describe me to listeners he used words like "barbaric, destructive, childish, uncivilized . . ." I thanked him very sincerely. I was thrilled with that attention and description from this educated man. It's not every day you get such flattery from someone educated far beyond his own intelligence.

I recall something I had learned in the writings of Sigmund Freud, in which he noted, "the concept of revenge is seen, at best, as a childish coping mechanism to keep darker forces at bay, and, at worst, as a manifestation of serious psychic illness." By Sigmund, he's right.

Today, the people who study such things about other people think that the 1980s will be known by historians as the Age of Mean. Since the '70s were known as the Me Decade, the '80s will be known as the Mean Decade. Proof? Have you heard some nitwit TV preacher refer to AIDS as God's punishment of homosexuals? Seen some hardcore punkers slam-dancing? Told any Challenger jokes? An hour after the shuttle exploded? The Reaganistas?

When did *Newsweek* do a cover story on "The New Cruelty," or when did David Letterman start that new feature called "Cruel Pet Tricks?" Oh come, grow up, this is America. Norman Rockwell doesn't live here anymore.

To paraphrase Lamont Cranston's father, the weed of mean bears bitter fruit, i.e., bullies. Bullies come in all sizes, tempers, and ways of expressing their bullydom. With characteristic modesty I think of myself as a Bullybuster, someone who helps people get back at bullies, new and traditional.

Why do people want to get even? I think it's because we feel the world ought to operate fairly, and when it doesn't work that way, we react. Most people adopt the "helpless victim" or the "that's the way it is, hit me again" approach. That's the scared citizen who swallows the bully's challenge or the old person who stays inside his city apartment behind a door with three locks. The other response is to "take action," which means talking back, striking back, or, in our case, *Haydukery*.

While America is discovering the fun of revenge, we'll never get to the Big Leagues, though, to the level of the Turks, Sicilians, Mexicans, or Corsicans. To most Americans, revenge is fun, i.e., getting even. To the nasty Grown-Ups mentioned above it is serious lifetime, or deathtime, actually.

When I pooped and snooped as one of Uncle's mufti-clad nephews I worked with two "sergeants" whose names were "Smith," of course. I remember one of them telling me about a couple of the "indigenous personnel" with whom we worked in someone else's country. Here's what he advised: "Never, ever, get on their shit list, George. Those bastards will follow you into hell itself to get their revenge. If you die before they even the score, they'll dig up your dead body and piss all over it. If it takes till the day after forever, they'll get even with you."

Wonder where those indigenous dudes are today, now that we need them again?

Write to Me

Many of the friends and ideas for my revenge books pop up from radio talk shows I have done all across the U.S.A., Mexico, and Canada these past five years. By the way, one of the most fun shows I've done recently was with KFYI's John Geesey in Phoenix, Arizona. There are some funny and grand people in that town who listen to that station. Thanks to John — and to them — I had a blast. It's also nice having a couple of old friends in that town, even if they couldn't get through on the phones until after the show. My other big-time fun talk show was with WWWE in Cleveland; again, grand enjoyment.

In addition to the talk shows, I get a lot of mail from friends and other readers. I answer it all by myself, too. I wish I had a corresponding secretary, but who would work for me? I do enjoy hearing from old, faithful and friendly readers as well as the new kids. Partly because letters are fun, but also because I would like to do another book. So, if you have any ideas, suggestions, stunts, or tricks to share, please write and tell me all about them. Write to George Hayduke, P.O. Box 1307, Boulder, CO 80306. If you include a return address, I will write back personally. Also, please let me know what pen name you want me to use if I include your stunt in the next book, or, if you wish, I can use your real name. I don't know about you, but this stuff is truly fun for me, so let's share the laughs. Write.

When the question of doing another book did come up, one of my friends at Paladin Press mentioned a moving quote from Mohandas Gandhi: "If everyone took an eye for an eye, the entire world would be blind." But, as I pointed out, and not with a sharp stick, then everyone would be even. Hayduke as philosopher?

How to Use This Wonderful Book

I have arranged these subjects both by method and mark, listing them alphabetically. In addition to using the obvious subject headings, you can also do a cross-reference of your own. Or you can adapt a method listed for one mark for another mark or situation. Thus, these subjects become as versatile as your own imagination.

While this mix 'n match versatility is a standard item here, the personalized nasty touch is still the best. Another effective part of this business is the anticipation of further damage after your initial attack. This is grand psychological warfare.

General Advice

Throughout this book I make universal reference to the "mark," which is a street label hung on the victim, male or female, of a scam or con or act of vengeance. In our case, the mark is a bully — anyone or anything — who has done something unpleasant, foul, unforgivable or fatal to you, your family, your property, or your friends. Never think of a mark as the victim of dirty tricks. Think of the mark as a very deserving bully, a target for your revenge.

Before you study any of the specific sections of this book, read these next few vital paragraphs. They tell you how to prepare before going into action.

1. Prepare a plan.

Plan all details before you take action at all. Don't even ad-lib something from this book without a plan of exactly what you're going to do and how. If your campaign involves a series of actions, make a chronological chart, and then coordinate your efforts. Make a list of possible problems. Plan what you'll do if you get caught — depending upon who catches you. You must have every option, contingency, action, reaction, and evaluation planned in advance. Remember, time is usually on the side of the trickster. As Winston Churchill — who is one of my favorite heroes for many, many reasons — once said, "a lie gets halfway around the world before the truth even puts on its boots." Or, as that old Sicilian homily goes, "Revenge is a dish best served cold," which means don't strike while your ire is hot. Wait. Plan. Think. Learn.

2. Gather intelligence.

Do what a real intelligence operative would do and compile a file on your mark. How detailed and thorough you are depends upon your plans for the mark. For a simple get-even number, you obviously need less intelligence than if you're planning an involved, time-release campaign. Before you start spying, make a written list of all the important things you need to know about the target — be it a person, company or institution.

3. Buy away from home.

Any supplies, materials, or services you need must be purchased away from where you live. Buy far in advance and pay in cash. Try to be as inconspicuous and colorless as possible. Don't talk unnecessarily with people. The best rule here is the spy's favorite — a good operative will get lost in a crowd of one. The idea is for people not to remember you.

4. Never tip your hand.

Don't get cocky, cute 'n clever, and start dropping hints about who's doing what to whom. I know that may sound stupid, but some would-be tricksters *are* gabby. Of course, in some of the cases this will not apply, e.g., unselling car customers at the dealership, or other tricks in which the scenario demands your personal involvement.

5. Never admit anything.

If accused, act shocked, hurt, outraged, or

amused, whichever seems most appropriate. Deny everything, unless, again, your plan involves overt personal involvement. If you're working covert, stay that way. The only cool guy out of Watergate was G. Gordon Liddy; he kept his mouth shut.

6. Never apologize; it's a sign of weakness.

Normally, harassment of a citizen is a low-priority case with the police. The priority increases along with the person's socio-financial position in the community and with his or her political connections. If you are at war with a corporation, utility, or institution, that's a different ball game. They often have private security people, sometimes retired federal or state investigators. By habit, these people may not play according to the law. If you play dirty tricks upon a governmental body, prepare to have a case opened. But how hard it is followed depends upon a lot of factors. Understanding all this ahead of time is part of your intelligence planning before you get started in action.

The Eleven Commandments of Revenge

Thanks to my Apostle of Revenge, Dick Smegma, I humbly present for your perusal, belief, and adherence, the Eleven Commandments of Revenge. Stay faithful and you'll enjoy a lot of yucks without suffering the heartbreak of being caught.

1. *Thou shalt neither trust nor confide in anyone!*
    If you do, that person could eventually betray you. Even if it is a relative or spouse, don't tell them what you are up to. Implicated accomplices are OK.
2. *Thou shalt never use thine own telephone for revenge business!*
    Always use a public telephone or that of an unwitting mark so calls cannot be traced back to you or to someone who knows you.
3. *Thou shalt not touch revenge documents with thy bare hands!*
    Bare hands leave fingerprints! Wear gloves.
4. *Thou shalt become a garbage collector!*
    Once your victim places his trash outside his home/office for pickup, it is 100 percent legal for you to pick it up yourself. You can learn about

your victim by sifting through his old papers, etc. The pros do it all the time.

5. *Thou shalt bide thy time before activating a revenge plot!*
Give the victim time to forget about you and what he's done to wrong you. Getting even too soon makes it easier for him to discover who's doing it!

6. *Thou shalt secure a "mail-drop" address in another city!*
You don't want revenge mail being traced back to your residence/town, do you?

7. *Thou shalt learn everything there is to learn about thy victim!*
The best revenge schemes/plans are hatched by people who know their victim better than the victim knows about himself.

8. *Thou shalt pay cash all the time in a revenge plot!*
Checks, money orders, etc., can be traced back to you. Cash cannot!

9. *Thou shalt trade with merchants who have never heard of you!*
Do business with people only once when involved in a revenge plot. Possibly wear a disguise so they will have trouble identifying you in a legal confrontation.

10. *Thou shalt never threaten thy intended victim!*
Why warn your intended victim that you are going to get even? When bad things begin to happen to your victim, whether or not you caused them, your victim will remember your threat, and he'll set out to even the score with you.

11. *Thou shalt not leave evidence lying around, however circumstantial.*
If you are thought to be actively engaged in having fun at your mark's expense, the authorities may visit you. Thus, it would be prudent not to have any books by Hayduke or Chunder on your shelves at home or in the office.

11

Caution

The schemes, tricks, scams, stunts, cons, and scenarios presented here are solely for information and amusement purposes only. It would never, ever be my intent that you use this book as a working field manual or trickster's cookbook. I certainly don't expect that anyone who reads this book would actually ever do any of the things described here. I know that I never would.

This book is written solely to entertain and inform readers, not to instruct or persuade them to commit any nasty or illegal act. From my own mild disposition, I could hardly tell someone else to make any of these tactics operational.

There's an old Creole saying that sums it up well: *Weso geye kofias na dlo, e se dlo ki kuit li,* which means something like, "A fish trusts the water, and yet it is in the water that it is cooked."

Please read this book with that reference in mind. Remember, it's all in good clean fun, isn't it? (That was a rhetorical question.) And, now, gentle reader, with all of the preamble behind us, let's get on with the *fun!*

Additives

Although John was in Tempe, Arizona, when he told me about it, I believed him. Later, a doctor confirmed it; then I had my own medical advisor for this series, Dr. Chris Doyle, also verify it for me. Here's the story. A drug known as Urised, aka methylene blue, when ingested, turns the urine a bright, deep blue. It is medically harmless if directions are followed. However, if the mark has no idea he or she has ingested the stuff, the resultant blue piss might cause some psychic harm to the personality's well-being. It could be great fun for you to try on some mark. Dr. Doyle says it would be fairly easy to administer in powder form. He did caution against massive overdose, however.

Airlines

If you think my old Panama pal, Lt.C. Mac, was irritated at Eastern, or that Syd Prine was pissed off at his airline, listen to what Bonnie Parker III did when an airline lost her luggage for the second consecutive time in two flights.

"After playing the harried lady executive, followed by the coy flirt, then, by the pissed-off business traveler, all to no avail, I recalled something in one of your books, George. Never had roadkill looked so good," Ms. Parker told me one evening.

"My boyfriend thought I was really nuts when I made him take me out to hunt some obnoxious roadkill, which we quickly found, it being early spring. I gathered it into a big bag, took it home and stuck the plastic bag in my freezer. When the roadkill was good and hard, I wrapped it a bit more and stuffed it into an old suitcase I bought at Goodwill. I put tags on that suitcase in the name of an old, old boyfriend I hated and took it to the airport to check it on the next flight of *that* damned airline to my least favorite city, presenting my own ticket that I had bought moments ago in my old ex-boyfriend's name (using initials, dummy).

"With the frozen roadkill-filled suitcase checked on the plane, I then cancelled my ticket, cashed it in, and left. The bag would arrive and as it would be unclaimed, *Dipshit Airlines* (not their real name) would have to store it."

Doesn't Ms. Parker III think well, for a normal person?

Alarm Clocks

Everyone knows someone whose intellectual humor delights in rousting you out of bed at times you would prefer to be deep into the Land of Nod. Shauna from Phoenix has an alarming way of ringing in some revenge for these dastardly dips. Considering that most are friends, roomies, or others with whom you have close association, this is fairly easy. Borrow or otherwise obtain seven or eight cheap, loud alarm clocks and secret them all around the mark's abode — all within easy listening distance of where mark sleeps — *after* you have set each clock's alarm to go off in sequential order about four or five minutes apart.

Another idea for the semi-engineering minded came in a strange letter with a German postmark and signed simply Hun. What you do is basically the same type of revenge technique, only you open up the alarm clock if it is the older, wind-up, or geared one. Once there you change the pin settings of the alarm so that it is an hour or two ahead or behind that of what it shows on the face. If you're not technically minded, says Hun, you may just cut the bell connector or disable the bell/ringer wire. Either way, the premature, late, or lack of alarm dings the mark.

Funny, I thought it was the Swiss stereotype who doctored clocks?

Animal Scent

Hunters know deer musk masks human odor in the woods. Bob from Newport News has another use in which you make the mark's clothing, car, or furniture smell like a deer in heat. Bob writes: "A two-ounce bottle of the stuff applied to the mark's car seat and ceiling pads will render the vehicle an olfactory disaster area. If the mark locks the car, just use a large hypodermic needle to insert through the door weather stripping and squirt away."

Another good sport, Lucy Gagette, told me that the same product applied in liberal fashion to the bedding or eating area of your mark's pet cat or dog can promote some wonderfully antic animal psychoses. Perhaps, you could squirt this stuff on the pant leg of your mark to create a bit of involuntary sodomy for the pet.

Answering Machines

The next time you are in your mark's home or business, take careful note if he has a telephone answering machine. If so, memorize the brand name (Sanyo, Code-A-Phone, etc.) and the model number.

Next, write to the manufacturer, explaining that you have lost or otherwise misplaced the owner's manual for that particular machine, and you'd like a replacement sent to you. Usually, the company will send you one free of charge, no questions asked.

Once you get the owner's manual, you can find out if the messages on the machine can be retrieved by remote control, using *any* touch-tone telephone. If so, you should be able to quickly determine the one- to three-digit code that allows you to play back your mark's personal messages, anytime you wish.

A word of caution, though, if you're going to do this intelligence-gathering bit: you will have to refrain from other means of messing with the machine, e.g., changing messages, etc. You don't want your mark to suspect that the answering machine has been compromised and that you're gathering goodies from it.

If you want to thank someone for this nice piece of advice, send a warm wave to Dick Smegma.

Apartments

This has to be Dr. Yaz's finest Yellow Brick Road. His mark lived in an apartment with a long, long hallway. The mark had to leave town for a business weekend. Somehow, Dr. Yaz and friends managed to appropriate a key to the apartment. And, with Dorothy and Toto's help, managed to lay an Oz number on the mark.

"We laid plastic covering down the long hallway, then under cover of night brought in many sacks of cement, which we mixed in the guy's bathtub, so we could pave his hallway. To finish off this boulevard, we painted the yellow line down the middle and scored the thing like bricks.

"As a finishing touch, we put up a big poster of Dorothy and friends on their Yellow Brick Road. It was on the door at the end of the hall so he'd see it at the end of his paved 'road.' "

One of the reasons Dr. Yaz and friends did this was because the guy was a jerk, plus, he annoyed young ladies who had no time for him.

Arrests

Using false identification in your mark's name, and, if necessary, your mark's "borrowed" car, get yourself arrested on a summary offense charge. Be polite and accept the summary. The twist is your false ID shows the mark's name with another address at some cutout mail drop. The trick happens when the hearing notification doesn't get to the mark, who obviously doesn't show up in court. He is tracked down through his license. He will really get arrested. By this time, the original cop probably doesn't remember what the mark looked like. So . . .

This is an involved stunt and has a minor degree of danger if you do it in a small, local jurisdiction. So, don't. I have seen it work twice in large, urban areas. Done properly, it creates a real nightmare for the mark.

Attacks on Haydukery

Early in 1986, a friend informed me that the State House of Legislators in Hawaii was considering two bills related to "harassment" and my reading of the text of those bills showed that they are aimed at good clean Haydukery.

Like my president, I don't have to take crap from anyone! So, like my president, I see this, as he does most everything he doesn't like, as an act of war!

If these odious pieces of dubious legislation pass, you can be sure that Hayduke will strike hard, fast, and often. And, unlike my own advice, I am openly warning my enemies. Gosh, I really am a nice guy. Reagan didn't even do that for Khadaffi Duck or however that Libyan Mad Dog spells his name. Mad Dog? Didn't that used to be a cheap, mind-busting wine?

Anyway, governments and the people who form them are rarely to be trusted. As the wonderful Linda Ellerbee has said, "Government is like a pizza because when it comes to morality, they can slice it any way they want and someone else will have to pay for the cheese."

Auto Dealers

For the first time, we hear from an auto dealer who got ripped off, but who succeeded in getting back at the costly customer. RepoMan from Denver told me that a local real estate dealer bragged how he never made payments on any car and always avoided repossession. Using a fake ID, our RepoMan set up an appointment for the deadbeat with some friends who claimed they were selling their big business, blinding the real estate jerk with $$$ signs. While he was trying to hustle the business friends, RepoMan took back his car. At a prearranged time, the friends excused themselves for a brief conference, and left the office — which was not theirs — got in their own car and drove to their home 175 miles away, after calling local police to report a "breaking and entering" at that office. One wonders how long the real estate schmuck sat there before the police arrived and what he did when he eventually went out to where he'd parked "his" car?

Auto Keys

Sometimes the key to getting back at your mark is simple. As Major General K. Oss relates, "I have gotten hold of my mark's keys and simply filed off a point or two on each key, rendering them useless."

A friend of mine pulled this stunt on his girlfriend after she locked him out of "their" apartment over some misunderstanding about lust or something minor like that. No problem, except for all of his extra clothes, money and so on that was kept in this apartment, for which he paid two-thirds of the rent. After she relented and they agreed to split, he was able to do this minor Dremel tool job on her keys. He says it was good for two days of aggravation and accusation on her part. He maintained perfect innocence and kept telling her to leave him alone. Great!

Automobiles

One of the nice things about being published all over the world is the calibre of minds I meet. That's why I was glad to hear from Mark Death in Brisbane, Australia. Mark's first idea was to get a plastic spray bottle like you might use for fine-spraying laundry or for window cleaning, but, this time, fill it with automotive brake fluid and spray it all over the paint finish of the vehicle. Two coats, says Mark Death, and the car's paint will start to peel and crack.

Mark's next idea is a cheaper and permanent improvement on the locking gas cap for your mark's car. You might simply wish to use epoxy to coat the threads of his regular gas cap and seal it on forever.

While working as a petroleum transfer engineer, aka gas pump jockey, in the colds of Western Canada a long time ago, Dr. Deviant found a neat way to get back at a nasty mark's car tires. The Dr. explains: "I would use a hypodermic syringe filled with a water and sugar mix. I would inject the mixture into the valve in hopes that the freezing water would wreck the tire or that the sugar would mess up the valve. It always worked."

Sometimes the most simple things can really annoy

and worry your mark. Larson Roberts likes it when his mark gets a new car or truck. "I spread a little puddle of oil under the new vehicle and smear a bit on the bottom of the engine or pan. The mark sees this and thinks he has a leak.

"Maybe the mark takes it back to the dealer and makes a pain of himself, or just pours in more oil at home. Hopefully, this overfilling will then cause real leaks and/or split seals," Larson says with a bright smile.

Over the past few years, I have heard many new ideas for filling a car with water and/or aquatic life. Until my Central American friend Bicho Cocha told me about this one incident, I had no idea someone would go to all of this trouble. According to Bicho, on their second date, it seems that the car owner decided he owned the sexual conduct of the young lady involved, due to meals and drinks. She did not agree. They finally reached an unhappy impasse, which he finally resolved by tossing her into the restaurant/motel swimming pool — in all of her finery — after she'd refused to go to bed with him. He also tossed their meals at her in the pool.

Better than even was the only way to go. She decided to create a Car Aquarium, and here is what she did. After extensive research, she learned where he parked his car, when it would be most open to attack, for how long, and with what effect.

Next, she opened the car and began to fill it in with rocks, plants (both real and plastic), and some tree limbs. Next, she shut the doors and sealed them with caulking. She then forced a hose into a window seal and ran a whole lot of water. She filled the car to the top of the window and left immediately.

As an added attraction, she alerted the local news media — especially television — about this odd car aquarium, tying it with some local, well-known charity, at the first pay phone she found.

Thanks to Dick Smegma I finally found out how

the term "bomb" became associated with automobiles. Here's how. It seems a plant supervisor not only stole a work improvement idea from two workers and claimed it as his own, but he also docked time unfairly from one of their pals because of a personal snit they'd had. Appeals and conversation on righting the wrongs never got beyond his own uncaring personality. He threatened suspensions, then firings.

Remember those five-gallon glass wine bottles and/or those huge bottles used upside down in office water coolers? These chaps got one of those and spent the next week filling it, instead of their urinal. Using a funnel, one fellow even managed to defecate in it several times as he had the runs badly. As a finale, another one ate the usual mix of pizza, vegetable soup and beer, then made himself vomit into the bottle.

Capping it tightly, they took this horrible mess to the supervisor's apartment complex and lugged it to the roof. Prior to doing so, they had determined that the boss parked his car head-on to the building and spotted the location. To aid in their aim, they spray-painted his windshield with phosphorescent paint which would show up in the dark — it being nighttime, of course.

Hoisting the huge bottle full of yukiness to the ledge, they lined up on their target with the care of a precision bombing crew. After making aiming allowances which a friendly engineer had calculated for them, they let it go over the edge. The bathroom bomb roared on toward the target.

The *crash* and *splash* had to be heard to be believed, one of the men told Dick. It smashed right through the windshield-target and exploded inside the car, showering the fermenting mixture of effluvia, excrement, and vomit everywhere in the vehicle's interior.

The car was less than six months old and was totally trashed. It was sold to a junkyard for parts — a $9500 Buick that brought less than $600 in return. The mark's insurance company refused to pay because of a technical error the guy had made in his coverage in an attempt to cheat the company. They said at work he became a beaten man and soon asked for a transfer. Bully for the bombers!

In another case of bully-busting, Zongie was afraid of his wife. A real termagant, she used to nail his ass every two weeks or so. Looking like Lyle Alzado in drag, she had only one pride and real love — her car, which she insisted on being hers and only hers. Bob from Newport News helped Zongie. Bob recalls, "We used Zap, one of the new acrylic cements for aircraft hobbyists, to stick the wipers to her car windshield. The best part was that she burned up the motor and had to get another one. She blamed it on vandals. In a way she was right."

Bob said their next stunt was a scientific experiment, "to see how long an automatic transmission will function with its cooling tubes crimped between the transmission and the radiator. In our one test, with 'Godzilla's' car, it took 15 miles to overheat the transmission, we figure. It seized and quit at 20. It happened when she was coming home from work on a fairly remote part of the roadway and she had to hike two miles to call for help."

Bob reports that when she asked Zongie for repair money, he reminded her she had always insisted it was her car. She paid. She may have gotten the point, too, as she started to act a bit more kindly to Zongie.

As an afterthought, Bob related that four tablespoons of common black pepper in an auto radiator will clog most of the cooling passages, causing almost immediate overheating. He said that will be their next zinger for Mrs. Zongie if needed.

Aunt Barby's been a friend of creative Haydukery for years, part of the price of living with the conductor of the Mount Lebanon Wind Symphony. Cutting off the quest for a motive, she gets directly to the right recipe that is without a doubt ideal for vehicular vermin, i.e., your mark and his car.

"It's quite simple," she says innocently, "you just add a cup or so of Minute Rice to the radiator of your mark's car. Not only have you gotten even, but you can even grain and bare it."

I think she meant something about shooting a moon. On the other hand, have a rice day with this.

Our recipe file of car radiator additives is piling up faster than vote fraud charges in a Mexican election. Krazy K adds dried beans, peas, or corn starch to our arsenal of additives. He also notes that we consider salt, too, as a long-term corrosive. In addition, Krazy K says you can add some fun things to the windshield washer tank as well, e.g., liquid detergent soap, ink, motor oil.

As an additive to the zapped windshield stunt to Mrs. Zongie's car, Dr. Deviant suggests you mix some alcohol solution in with the super glues to keep them from drying out. Seal well until needed, and then dump the solution into the windshield washer fluid reservoir of the mark's car.

Another nice additive for windshields was suggested by a bevy of beautiful pranksters, including Allen, Todd, Sally, Kristina and Chuck. The simple cure is to smear a lot of Vaseline on the mark's car windshield. It is a great dust and bug catcher, and otherwise makes clear driving rough.

Here's one we're borrowing from the old house, where this stunt was first used by some friends and me back in the early '50s on a nasty neighbor, before we had ever heard of the word "mark." It's the old dead-animal-in-the-home-heater-vent trick. Why not do the same thing with a mark's car? Put a dead squirrel or rat in the heater duct of the vehicle in winter? I don't know why not, so go do it.

What? Whaddaya mean I have no class or sophistication? I also have friends in Italy, too. Andrea Grosso wrote to tell me that Hayduke is big fun in Italy. He also passed along some stunts he has pulled in his country.

At one time a snobby acquaintance made fun of Andrea for learning English. He hassled him about it a whole lot. Andrea waited until his critic was in a bistro trying to impress some of the local talent to go for a ride in his new car. In the meantime, Andrea was unloading an entire cupful of stinky garlic sauce in that car's heating vent. It was a winter evening in Turin, Andrea added.

Andrea said the mark and his girl came out and got into his car. He started the engine and, in a few seconds, obviously, the heater fan as well. The car door flew open and the young woman exited, screaming curses and insults at the mark while she wiped stinky, saucey shrapnel from her coat.

Another good way to spruce up your mark when he or she is all dressed up with someplace nice to go is to put photo copier dry chemical in the air conditioning vents of the mark's car. This stuff really smears, especially if it gets warm and wet. Several readers suggested this idea.

Mr. Justice says that a cigar is more than a good smoke; it's also a fine way to bugger your mark's car. Take a good-sized, cheap cigar and slit the outer leaves to help the unraveling process. Then simply dump the stogie in the gas tank of the marked car. It may take weeks for the tobacco to shred into small enough bits to flow at least partially into the gas line, with predictable results.

Like herpes, this stunt just keeps giving. Mr. Justice explains that the mark "takes the car in and gets the gas line cleared, but there is obviously more cigar in the tank. Unless the mark gets the tank cleaned, there will be more clogging."

Awards

A good sharp shot to the ego will double your mark over with embarrassment. You'll need access to a printer if you carry this one all the way. Make up a bogus award and arrange to have the certificate presented to your mark at some public gathering, like a company dinner or party. Make sure the local newspaper gets a copy of the story and has a photographer there. After all of the publicity, you might notify the organization that was supposed to have made the award about the imposter. This works well if your mark actually has some sort of association with the organization in question.

An abridged version of the same stunt cuts out the elaborate presentation and goes directly to the newspaper, i.e., simply give them a new release about the bogus award. If you make this big enough or serious enough, e.g., an honorary Ph.D. degree from some actual university, you could next tip off the newspaper's investigative reporter about this cad who is trying to pull a Janet Cooke on them. Nobody gets more indignant than a newspaper reporter who thinks some ordinary citizen is trying to take a literary dump in the hallowed halls of journalism. They're sensitive because it happens all the time. They've even established a name for this brand of hoaxing and paid lying. It's called public relations.

Banks

A really snooty bank in a college town bought its way onto campus, opening a branch in the student union, by spreading cash both over and under the table. Everyone in the Establishment was happy, drinking well at the trough of greed. Meanwhile, as usual, the students got to stand at the other end of this financial digestive system, i.e., they got shat upon.

The bank soon instituted outrageous service charges for all sorts of routine transactions. They got nasty. They acted like they were, gee, part of the university administration. Some students decided enough was too much.

You have to realize that these students were mutants. They weren't like the collegiate vegetables, Falwell Freaks, Geeks, Greeks and other brain dead Pre-Yuppies who fester our campuses today. These mutant kids cared about honesty and fairness.

They got a lot of friends to go along with it because they promised free beer for each and every deposit/withdrawal slip presented that night. And, here's what they did.

They got a *huge* line of students, armed with $10,

33

$20 and $50 bills, to go into the bank and open an account of some type. Then, each student would go back out to the end of the line, move forward, come back in and make a withdrawal. The bookkeeping department was in a shambles, its computers in a burnout frenzy. Bank officers were called in from the country club bar or the golf course. Chaos. Wonderfulness. Reform? That was asking for too much. Instead, they called the police and closed their bank for the rest of the day. But, stay tuned . . .

Billboards

Billboards, the most obnoxious form of advertisement because it uglies and clutters our countryside, deserve any and all of the fun we can do to them. William Board, who has a grand name, is a Truth in Advertising spokesman in California who claims to have altered more than 15 billboard ads in 1985 and 17 more in 1986. He says he's never been caught in three years, despite police stakeouts demanded by uptight Establishment heavies.

Board claims many cops are on his side and have helped him by tipping him to troublesome stakeout sites. Most of his alterations are of a political nature involving nuclear energy, U.S. policy in Central America and California's most disgusting export, Ronald Reagan.

His usual MO is to scale the billboard and artistically alter the wording or picture on the board to satirize his mark. His ethical rules demand that he attack only those who attack or victimize others. According to most press accounts, William Board is a bit of a folk hero in that region.

Bitchy Calls

Everyone who's ever worked anywhere the public can call to complain has faced the Bitchy Call — you know, taking the red ass for something you didn't do, know nothing about or have any control over, anyway. Marching to the relief of beleaguered timorous telephonics is Joe Prosnick with his solution.

"You answer the telephone and as soon as you establish that it's a certified bitchy call, you start to get snide and abusive. If asked, you identify yourself with the name of an employee who passed away recently."

Joe adds, "I'm a newspaper photographer and we get a lot of crackpots who call to bitch about what we publish. We all use the name of one of our colleagues who died several years ago — then, we abuse the crackpot. The loony calls the editor and relates how rude and awful this Mr. Blank was."

Most editors are used to crank calls and figure the bitchy caller has made it all up, and they deliver another return message. By definition, a bitchy phone call is regarded as one which is unreasonable, shrill, demanding, whiney, insulting, illiterate, or from a politician or a TV preacher.

Body Fluids and Semifluids

According to the McGeary Codicil to the Panama Canal Treaty, "Vomitus is not littering." That's all very good for the diplomatic crowd, but it doesn't stand a very tall statute when someone performs bodily functions in your car — a classic tale of many American males of high school age. Nanker Phelge wrote to tell me that he had a good way of really paying back someone who not only barfed in his car, but was so drunk that he also voided his bladder at the same time.

"This brainless creep kept telling me he was OK. I wanted to stop to let him go to the side of the road, but, *noooo*, he was fine," Nanker says. "A minute later he unloads it all in the backseat of my car. Nice. The next day he was blaming me for the whole thing, muttering about how my driving made him sick. He was feeding us a line, so I decided to feed him back.

"I have this formula for 'Golden Shower Gravy' which makes a fine substitute for regular, therapeutic chicken soup. Start with some dehydrated chicken soup mix, then add pee to fill and flavor. Bring to a hard boil, thicken with a small amount of flour, stir for one minute, cool slightly, then serve to your mark."

Nanker did this the following day in the mark's own home . . . then, told him about it fifteen minutes after the guy had scarfed down the soup.

"At least this time he decorated his own place," Nanker closed.

Boomboxes

This teenage punk, wearing the livery and hairstyle of his ilk, sauntered along West Fourth Street carrying a monster box, the volume of its rock music matching the level of a Concorde on takeoff. He gazed at Walter Zapper, walking in the opposite direction.

"If you don't like it, Square, what you gonna do about it?" The punk felt secure. He was mistaken.

Walter had his right hand inside his raincoat pocket. In the palm of his hand was a black object about the size of a pack of cigarettes. Walter pressed the thumb switch. The noise from the box stopped abruptly. What came out of the box now was not rock music, but a wisp of smoke. The rat didn't know his radio had been zapped by a radio beam from Zapper's raincoat pocket. All he knew was that the wiring and insulation were burning.

No, it's not a joke or a made-up dream. An MIT electronics engineer, Walter Zapper is quite real and his hobby is using his talents wisely and well to take away, electronically, as many of life's annoyances as possible. Walter is somewhat of a legend to a few folks in New York City, where he also has a device which trashes automobile horns, one for manipulating the ON/OFF DUTY signs of taxi cabs, and yet another for controlling the electric windows of automobiles.

Bovine Effluvia

I was going to use *Bullshit* for this category, when my editor gently reminded me that we now live in religiously conservative times and that the pious pulpit-pullers would probably flock to the bookshops and torch my tomes if I used anything but God-Squad approved language. Thus . . .

I learned about this product from Tom, a friend in the newspaper business who quickly produces it for defensive use when cornered by what passes as the sports editor at his newspaper. You must understand that the target of my friend's spray is the most obnoxious person in the universe — trust me, I've met him.

This six-ounce spray can has a delightful label clearly stating *Bullshit Repellent* and you can use it to disperse even the most stubborn and prolific verbal excrement, e.g., witness my friend's use of it to vanish the idiot editor. See the *Sources* section for further details.

Seriously, though, some enterprising chaps have been reading my books. I'm happy to report that more and more honest American business folks are selling ideas founded upon my philosophy, and, ahem, ideas. I love it. The latest is a *Crap-o-gram,* which is just about as it sounds. These folks will send your vexing pain in the ass of a mark a nasty, insulting message along with a gift-wrapped box of fake cow manure. See *Sources* for details.

Bumper Stickers

I travel a lot and see many bumper stickers. I also have had samples sent to me by readers and friends. Some of them aren't very pleasant, although I found most of them to be funny. Some were so obnoxious that my editor refused to allow them in my last book. "They offend people," I was told. Hey, I thought that was my point. Oh well . . .

Here are a few that may be less offensive, but no less visible, on the back deck of someone's vehicle. To avoid offending the pressure-sensitive, I will try it this time with your imagination's cooperation. We'll play complete the sentence. I furnish the first part of the bumper sticker and you use your own mind, creativity or nastiness to complete the statement. Here we go...

MICROWAVE THE _____!
I'D RATHER BE KILLING _____!
JESUS WAS _____!
I _____ MY _____!
I MURDERED MY _____!
PISS ON _____!

That's the ticket then — now you can make up your own. See *Sources* for the places to print them for you.

Burials

The Philly Phantom has a great idea for deadhead marks, the type of jerk, if the world were a bottle of mouthwash, your mark would be a case of halitosis. Apparently, the Philly Phantom knows people like that. He writes, "When much else failed to get a reaction from this jerk, I finally called four different burial plot companies and set up interviews for my mark at his home. I later did this for a burial vault sales company, too. Maybe, he got the idea someone was after him?" Actually, in Philadelphia, that's a fairly good assumption, right, Mr. Bruno?

Camp Counselors

After the last two books, I heard from all sorts of camp counselors who wanted ideas on how to get back at the obnoxious little peckerheads who infest summer camps because their parents wanted the time free from these past sexual mistakes. Actually, Jason Vorhees was first in line with ways to get back, but, he's found his own groove, so we turn to Captain Video, who, in addition to his experiences in minor league baseball, is also a camp counselor.

"It's an old trick, but fun. If you have a truly rotten kid who won't adjust to the regular drill and rule, some night fill his hand with shaving cream, then tickle his nose. If that doesn't work to settle him, check out his shampoo.

"If it is white or cream-colored, replace it with condensed milk or Elmer's glue thinned with solvent, or use Nair. If it is orange-colored, you can use cooking oils and jam," says Capt. Video.

Capt. Video says that you should not get caught or even put under suspicion for revenging the kids. "Remember, camping isn't fun, it's a business for someone and you don't want to piss off the director and get fired. Always try to get your pranks blamed on the second worst kid in the outfit."

Cassette Tapes

According to many of my music phreak phans, mass-produced music cassettes are getting worse in terms of quality disregard, i.e., more and more turn up defective. How to get even? Macho from New York City talked with a store manager who refused him a refund or even a credit for a truly defective tape he returned. It went like this:

MACHO: This tape's defective.

MGR: It's open. How do I know you didn't just copy it and are now returning it — to cheat me?

MACHO: Simple, play the tape for yourself. See, it's defective.

MGR: No credit. Take your tape and leave.

Macho did. But, he later came back with a hand-held portable magnet and proceeded to "help the manager by making certain nobody would ever victimize this manager's tapes by copying them."

According to Macho, a friend who worked in a nearby store told him that the manager had been having some bad scenes with punks and other badasses who obviously had brought defective tapes, too, as in *nothing* was on these new tapes . . . no music, nothing.

Castration

Don't only threaten to de-ball a mark, show him "proof" of past surgical escapades! Send him a brief, untraceable note explaining in detail how you castrated another jerk who messed with your life. Enclose two dried prunes or slightly made-up or disguised apricots in the letter. You might stain the end with some actual blood and let dry a few days before mail delivery to your mark.

Ms. Lisa was bullied at a party, followed home and bothered further by a wanna-be romeo with all the suavity of a puke-ridden leisure suit. After three civilized attempts to get him to leave, she told him she was calling the police. He said he would hurt her body, badly. Since she knew his name and address, she locked herself in her room and did call the police. One week later, she had her good friend from an old line Corsican family complete the stunt mentioned in the previous paragraph. I think this mark is now selling trusses to penguins at the South Pole.

In another instance, a lady told me about a friend who had narrowly missed a nasty rape by some drunken "students/athletes" from the local state university, well known as a football factory. In turn, one of her friends knew how to get back at the potential rapists, chemically.

She told me, "There is a very nasty chemical which is available legally which will turn a rapist into a eunuch very quickly with regular dosage. It does what our courts won't do — chemically castrate the rapist."

The product is available from an outfit known as BBN, see *Sources*.

Cement

Mr. Science came up with a good one from the halls of Ace McCutcheon High School. He says that an ounce of regular table sugar placed in 100 pounds of concrete cuts its bonding strength significantly.

Ace adds, "I read this in a consumer alert bulletin that the CIA was mailing to peasants in Nicaragua who might have this problem due to the Contra influx into their lives."

According to Ace and Mr. Science, the concrete mix's calcium combines with the sugar instead of carbon dioxide and you get calcium saccharate, which is soluble.

I've always wondered about that, but they say it really works.

Chemicals

Rooftop warfare comes easily in NYC and can lead to fun, as Chuck Slender tells me. From the twenty-third floor of a midtown building, he did just that, filling a large bottle with hydrochloric acid which he'd purchased in a pool supply shop. He then dropped in a few chunks of aluminum and capped the bottle tightly.

The combination of the two forms a very dark gas cloud that smells as bad as it looks. Chuck had a shill on the street below near the movie theater to which they owed a chemical revenge for the nasty it had done to him and his friends. When the crowd outside the theater was long and impatient, it was "bombs away."

Chuck says, "We let that sucker fall into the street right near the crowd. This huge, dark cloud formed out of the explosion and began to drift toward the crowd. My man on the street shouted *'Poison gas!'* and told the people to run for their lives."

The police and fire people were there in minutes, and closed the theater and several streets in the area for a two-hour period. Chuck and his friends, meanwhile, had gone elsewhere.

Thanks to Macho, our guerrilla advisor from NYC,

we now have a single source for a whole lot of disgusting chemicals with which you can do terrible things to your mark. Here is his shopping list:

1. *Rotten Eggs Scent.* This bargain carries the strong aroma of sulphur.
2. *Skunk Repellent.* Safely keeps skunks out of your yard.
3. *Dog/Cat Repellent.* Safely keeps dogs/cats from making messes in your yard.
4. *Skunk Scent.* Actual skunk essence. Its horrible, pungent odor is sure to linger on and on.
5. *"P" Scent.* Fermented fox urine. Smells musky and is stomach-turning.
6. *Fart Spray.* Absolutely the most disgusting odor imaginable. In an aerosol spray can, a one to two second burst will "perfume" a room thoroughly. Experiment *outdoors.*

According to Macho, all of these are available from On The Nose. (See *Sources* for details.)

There are other uses for chemicals which don't seem quite as nasty. For example, photocopying does more than just make its mark on the American literary scene, creating copyright bandits of us all. Thanks to my faithful researcher from Canada, Dr. Deviant, a new and positive use has come from these delightful machines.

He reports, "I worked in a reprographics department, where the copy machines are, and learned from personal experience that the dry toner used in most of the machines is really a pain to work with. If you get it on your skin, you must rinse it away with cold water immediately; if you use warm water, it bonds to your skin like it does to paper."

Oh, my, that info got Dr. Deviant's mind rolling. He suggested all sorts of uses for the chemical, which is easily available from office supply shops. It might be the second generation chemical of choice to mix in with powdered soap at a least favorite restaurant or plant washroom. Could it be molded into a bar of "home-made soap" now that homemade soap kits are cheaply available? Could it be mixed with bathwater perfumes and softeners? Could it replace the dye-in-the-shower-head from an earlier volume? Or, your turn now . . .

Coin-Operated Machines

Tired of being ripped off by her local car wash whose machine ate her quarters but refused to give her fair service, Little D grumbled to the absentee owner by letter, which was ignored. She found out the guy also owned a local Laundromat and that those machines were also ripping off people.

All of the coin-operated equipment had coin trays where you deposit your quarter in the round depression, then slide the handle in to deposit the coin and supposedly activate the process. Note that each tray has a hole in the coin tray to permit you to poke your finger up to retrieve your coin if you change your mind before the money goes into the machine.

Buy or borrow a number of small, cheap padlocks and lock one through the hole and edge of each coin tray on each machine in any place that is ripping off people, says Little D. It closes down the operation immediately, causing the mark lost revenue and even more irritated customers.

Dick Smegma has another solution. He suggests super-gluing slugs or actual coins into these coin trays, which also voids the operation.

College Bookstores

No kidding, I went through college, although it was 77 years ago. I remember that one of our biggest rip-offs then was buying new books from the campus bookstore, then, "selling" them back again at the end of the term for a pittance of the original price. It seemed a rip-off then, and, according to the students from whom I get calls and letters now, it is still the same old thievery. Here's my solution.

Pretend you're the instructor for a particular course. Call in, and then follow up with a memo on purloined or recreated memohead (see my earlier books on how to create these forms). Make it seem that "you" want to order a new book for the next semester. The store will do this, and the real prof will have no idea about any of this until the next semester. Your used book from the semester before will be very, very valuable to the students now taking the course. Your thanks for this idea go to "Two Radio Guys From Denver."

Computers

Some lonely people are so happy to get phone calls that they might be two minutes into the thing before they realize all the one-sided monolog is from a machine, a computer-generated call, usually from a business. When these machines are programmed to make a pitch and provide you the opportunity to respond to a recorder, Arizona Mary has a fun way to give them the business. She pretends she is a computer, too.

"It took a bit of study and practice, but I can now talk just like an electronic, machine-generated voice. I talk to the machine in machine-talk — varying my message, depending upon what it said to me. It's fun and can sometimes mess up the human who will have to listen to the other end of my lines."

A neighbor of Mary's is not so kindly. A hacker by serious hobby, he has a lock 'n trace device on his equipment that runs down the location and number calling him as a computer-generated "junk mail" call. If this becomes enough of a nuisance and he wishes to play get-even, he puts his own computer on the call-generation mode and ties it to the company's regular business line.

"This way, I can tie up their normal business line or

their 800 number for sales orders if it's long distance. It's a fun payback," according to Herr Hacker.

Condoms

New uses for the ubiquitous condom continue to pour in from tricksters who use rubbers for more than putting that macho circular indentation in their wallets. Our prolific Mr. Heffer from Missouri recalls some uses from his college days of bunk beds and not-so-considerate dorm colleagues.

"You know the bastards who party all night, then come in sloppy drunk, make noise, fart, vomit, all that?" It was a rhetorical question. "Here's my strike-back. Fill a large condom with about two gallons of cold water — yes, it will all fit. Elevate your mark's bed slightly at the bottom. Place the condom under the covers at the foot of the bed.

"The drunken mark slides in, breaks the condom and is flooded to the crotch with cold water. Hopefully, he will piss the bed at this point, too."

Mr. Heffer's alternative idea works with bunk beds. He says, "This time carefully — and, I stress carefully — place the water-filled rubber between the mattress and springs of the top bunk. The light needs to be out, of course, and you need to be sure your mark is in the lower bunk. It would help, too, if the mark's top-bunk roomie gets to bed after the mark. Great idea, huh?''

Contests

It's easy to either hold a contest or to enter a mark or someone in the mark's family in the contest. It's also a grand way to gain public ridicule for your mark. According to the renowned psychologist, Solly Barkloudly, people who are overweight, ugly, stupid, or all three, really are upset by this, despite what they may proclaim, or what you may read in the cheerleader press. You can use this to your advantage.

If your mark has a daughter who looks like a beach ball with arms, enter her in the Goodyear Blimp Lookalike Contest and inform the mark you have done so. If you have lazy or stupid people at the desks of your local newspaper or radio station, take advantage. Name the mark or someone in the mark's family as the "winner" of some award in a dubious, insulting contest. When in doubt, remember Les Nessman of the TV show *WKRP in Cincinnati?* Very realistic show — I worked at a radio station just like it for a year.

Contra Aid

To ease the hygiene problem facing El Presidente's favorite freedom fighters in their invasion of Nicaragua, Phyllis Schafly's Eagle Forum organization has donated "personal cleanliness kits" for distribution to our Contra surrogates who run their cross-border terrorist attacks from Costa Rica and Honduras. In each kit are breath mints, toilet paper, a Spanish-language Bible and "inspirational literature" featuring messages from El Presidente and Mrs. Schafly. No, I am *not* kidding you; it's all true.

Here is where Pablo Digno de Heno comes into this big picture. Not only does Pablo disagree with the Reaganista aggression against Nicaragua, he is also interested in doing what he can to defeat it. That is why Pablo's group has put together units of a subkit which he has infiltrated into Mrs. Schafly's parcels. Included in Pablo's subkits are:

- Small packets of marijuana imprinted with the Presidential seal and the logo, Reaganista Gold
- Two packets of condoms with instructions in Spanish saying "For prevention of future Contras left behind during pillage." The packets are signed with the

legend, "For a good time when in the U.S.A., call Phyllis Schlafly," which is followed by the Eagle Forum telephone number.

- A packet of wallet-sized color photos of Somoza with instructions for passing them out to villagers in Nicaragua.
- A document awarding the bearer an officer's commission in the Somoza National Guard.
- Conterfeit Nicaraguan cordobas (money) with Ronald Reagan's picture on each bill.

Pablo estimates that several hundred of his kits got through, disguised with the real units, and found their way into Contra hands.

Who is Pablo Digno de Heno? He's a U.S. Navy vet. A pacifist? Not on your life! This man's a serious collector of serious right-wing causes. But, he just doesn't like to see stupidity repeat itself.

Controversy Clearing House

Thanks and a tip of the Hayduke homburg to Vonnie Bruce for this grand idea to clutter a mark's mail and telephone with controversial communication. She based it upon a woman with whom she once shared an apartment. The woman in question was a legend in her own mind and spent hours verbally reminding everyone how great she was. Vonnie's big chance came during one of those people-in-the-street interviews which a large radio network played nationally.

"They asked me about abortion and I replied, 'Americans haven't been told all the facts about secret, tax-paid abortions for the mistresses of TV stars and politicians,'" Vonnie related. "I went on whetting audience interest for about twenty more seconds, and then said, 'If you want more information on these secret, illegal abortions that you're paying for with your tax dollars, contact. . .'"

At this point, Vonnie gave the audience her ex-roommate's home address and telephone number as the information source. She says that three radio stations called the confused markess for more interviews, and she was getting dozens of calls and letters daily.

This same routine will work for many other types of issues. Just pick something which is very emotional, controversial and polar. And be sure you are the "voice of an authority" on the subject. Reporters, radio and TV people are very gullible with stuff like this (see *Media*).

Corporate/
Institutional

Obviously, the ideas here can be used elsewhere and otherwise, but for now they go under this category. I included this category because a lot of talk-show callers asked me how and what to do with nasty co-workers. Here are some suggestions.

You can always order printing, photography, repairs, or other types of services for the mark and/or the mark's department. The success here is to keep each individual order small, as in $200 or under. The range of revenge here is limited only by your imagination. One caller told me she ordered her mark six different luxury items that would look suspicious to a corporate comptroller or auditor, e.g., Omaha steaks, personally monogrammed clothing, booze, etc.

Everyone in personnel departments worries about not violating various privacy and other related laws when it comes to employee evaluations or job applications. A Hayduker spends time thinking of ways to include illegal and obnoxious items on such forms. After completing your modified form, see if you can bootleg it into the system where it will show up randomly.

Or, as an alternative, you can prepare *and* complete

such a form for someone else, then submit it to the appropriate office for processing. See them go bonkers when they discover the awful items. It might be fun to use a secondary mark as the person "who" filled out the form.

You need to include items of specific information on these forms that flagrantly violate racial, sexual, ethnic, religious and privacy laws. Do it grossly; if they wish to know your sex I am sure you can furnish crude words for that, too.

Creative Editing

Go on, admit it. You've always had a hankering to play Steven Spielberg, Chuck Barris, or one of those other biggie movie producers. When you act on that urge, do it so as to win an award for embarrassment to your mark. Kick him right in the Oscars.

Everyone is into home movies or home videos these days. Your idea is to get hold of your mark's prize films or videos and do some creative editing. It would be great fun to insert scenes with John Holmes and his Mr. Johnson doing fun things with Serena, Seka or Jesse St. James. You can edit in a few flash frames, so it looks like subliminal seduction, or you can cut in longer scenes for total outrage. Or, put out a casting call to some of your more outrageous and less-inhibited friends so you can produce your own blue loop to be included with the mark's family scenes.

Later, when the offending footage is shown during family gatherings, plan to have or include some shill in the audience to either yuk-up and encourage the mark's guilt or to berate him for such poor taste. This scam works wonderfully well with some person who is very obnoxious about dictating his fundamental religious beliefs on you. Or, you might use one of these brain-locked zombies to add to your own mark's woes if he is not a zealot.

Credit Cards

If you bother to read the back side of your bank-generated credit card, you will notice a policy about disputed charges. That refers to a situation in which you dispute a charge item or amount on your bill, or that a company did not credit you for a return, never sent the merchandise to you, or whatever. There are formal steps, involving only your writing a letter, to create an "in dispute" situation for that transaction and amount only, meaning you don't have to pay until the dispute is resolved.

Perhaps, you can find out that your mark has a disputed transaction. If you know the mark's card number, you can easily call the bank and tell the credit card service representative that everything is okay for the deal, that "you" want the dispute status removed and it's alright to charge that amount to "your" account. By the time the mark catches up with the affair at the next billing cycle, it will be far too late for a simple resolution.

Cult Stuff

While sharing a few glasses of Scotch 'n Bile with Chuck Manson down in Dallas last fall, we got to discussing his old family ties in California. He told me that one of his ladies came in one visiting day to pass along a keen idea. It seems that one of the late Nixon administration's top White House press people had recently been reborn as a Manson Family member and had this thought.

"He said it would be a really peachy-keen idea to sneak into your mark's office or home and replace all of the family portraits and pictures displayed there with group photos of the Manson Family itself, or members of the family engaged in bizarre sex acts," Chuck told me.

What? You thought Chuck was still in jail? Naive, naive, naive. Those California cultists stick together. Actually, following a highest level political decision, Chuck was secretly freed and replaced in prison by a "specially trained CIA lookalike." Someone has plans for Chuck both in Central America and with the 1988 reelection campaign.

Customs

One of the neat things about the Customs Service today is that they will investigate almost anything, regardless of what it is, as Dick Smegma so informed me. He adds that if you know that your mark is returning to this country on a specific date, including flight number, airline and arrival time, all you have to do is get a message to local customs officials at the arrival city informing them mysteriously that "John Mark" will be attempting to smuggle "something" into the country. You need not give out any additional details.

When your mark arrives, regardless of who he is and who he knows, I can guarantee you that he will be given a *thorough* searching. The more the mark protests and gets pissed about it, the more persistent do the customs people become, only they will remain maddeningly polite about it all. The best part is, even if the mark appears to be clean, if the customs inspector's suspicions are aroused, a file will be opened and this beef will follow the mark on each departure and arrival.

Dead Animals

Even without Stephen King, pet cemeteries are a big business. But I can easily think of other uses for dead animals. "Advertise for them and buy their bodies." In every telephone directory you can spot an ad for an animal disposal and/or rendering company. Why not set up your mark in the same business? A series of small ads in the local newspapers will do it. In addition to listing the telephone number to call, with business hours you know are inconvenient to the mark, you can also tell people about your special "Bring Right Down to the Plant" feature, listing the mark's home address.

This gives new meaning to the concept of 101 things to do with a large, dead plow horse.

Dogs

He is a former NYC cop who now lives in Sarasota, Florida, and he likes dogs "unless they bark at night or dump in my yard — but, I'd never really harm them like some folks do." Instead, he makes a tasty treat, involving a little meatball which surrounds a lot of canine-sized portions of Ex-Lax.

"The next step is to make sure you shut them in the owner's yard, house, apartment, or automobile. Or, if you have another mark in your neighborhood, you can leave the soon-to-be-pooping pup with him."

Relax, animal lovers, this really does not hurt the animal, only cleans it out thoroughly and messily. Just be certain you give a child-sized portion. Who knows, maybe the mutt has worms and this will help clean that out, too. And, you can always think of your mark trying to clean that up.

Our ex-cop reminds, "This works great for the mark who lets the dog roam all over the place. You're helping out by taking the doggie home."

Doorknobs

We call this one the Skull's Wake-Up call from MP school. He noticed how many of his rotten mark enemies — really bad people he needed to get even with in a hard fashion — left their porch lights on all evening. Perfect. All you need is a light bulb adapter with an outlet on it, plus an extension cord that's been stripped of six inches of insulation at one end.

Wear insulated gloves, unscrew the lightbulb, replace it with the adapter, and then fit the bulb back in the adapter. Carefully wrap the stripped, bare wires around the mark's doorknob. Carefully plug the plug into the adapter. You've now left a shocking wake-up call for when the mark opens the front door.

At this point, Skull says you're free to ring the doorbell, knock loudly, or just let nature take its course. Your options depend on many factors about who will be approaching that live door, when, and from what side.

74

Drugs

Planting drugs predates even old me. But, because he is an ex-cop, Mr. Justice has a more pragmatic twist to the stunt. The ingredients you need are some oregano, spearmint shavings, and some small manila or glassine envelopes of the type favored by stamp collectors and drug dealers. You mix these ingredients well and pop them into a hiding place in your mark's car. Try for something really exotic, like under the seat. Now comes the fun.

Mr. Justice explains, "Call the local police and give them some imaginary name or the name of one of the mark's friends — be prepared with a real address, too. After you have identified 'yourself,' tell police that Mr. Mark is dealing drugs out of his car. Personally you don't care about a little grass for adults, but now he's selling PCP and bad coke to little neighborhood kiddies."

Mr. Justice's next instructions are to hang up and split the entire area with great, but not suspicious, haste. The police will quickly send a zone car to the mark's address — which you gave them — and a search will be made of his car. A field test may come out negative, but

75

the minty smell of "PCP-laced grass" will merit a further investigation "downtown." This means your mark will be taken into custody and the ingredients will have to be lab-tested.

Mr. Justice says the same scam will work if you want to make your mark out as a numbers runner. All you need here are some homemade or real numbers slips and some amount lists. In both cases, not only will the police be interested, but so might those who really do deal in drugs and numbers. Perhaps, then, some other enforcers will come to visit your mark and discuss his new business.

Ecotage

Years ago, when concerned people started saying *hell no* to the greedy grabbers of profitable progress, somebody combined the terms ecology and sabotage to come up with *ecotage*. My own mentor, Edward Abbey, invented the term monkeywrenching in his book, *The Monkey Wrench Gang*, and it's been quite a progression. That's why I consider David Foreman a soil brother of ours. David publishes *EarthFirst!*, the magazine of the environmental activist. He also has written a field manual called *Ecodefense: A Guide To Monkeywrenching*, which is basically how to sabotage land rapists.

I gladly share the beliefs and dreams of these fine folks and happily share anything they can use from the Haydukery involved in my books. Probably the best endorsement I ever heard for them came from a public relations whore for the logging industry who said, "Foreman's publications all carry a disclaimer about using the ideas, but, that's like handing out hand grenades and saying, 'we don't advocate you use them, but here they are.'" Isn't that great?

Or, as my own great pal, Uncle George, might say,

"By God, let's turn the Alaskan pipeline over and see what's on the other side."

So far they sound like my kind of Give 'em Hell Harry Truman ass kickers; then, I called David Foreman. It seems he has a staff of flunkies, one of whom sounded uptight as he fussed about "David's image and associations." My request for information and a copy of Foreman's manual for review in *this* book would "have to be checked and considered."

A day or so later, one of the foremost of the Foreman minions called back to refuse all cooperation with me. I was told that association with me and my book would not serve in Mr. Foreman's best interest. I was crushed.

Still, I believe in what David Foreman is doing, as our roots are common and he plucked the weed of "monkey wrenching" from the same garden of ecological warfare (aka ecotage) as I did. My only regret is I can't give him a fat, wet kiss, right on the lips, in front of his horrified court of staff remoras.

Excrement

For some reason I have always liked this word. Perhaps, it goes back to Miss McDowell's trowel. I wonder if Howard or Jack would remember? Mick, do you recall? Anyway, Rick has a new use for human effluvia, and that is to smear it on the air conditioner intake of an apartment or office. I wonder if one uses a spatula or other special applicator? Otherwise, it could be very uncomfortable trying to squat in there — oh, never mind.

Excrement has always been a fashionable material for terrorizing a deserving target. Our own OSS and the British SOE used it in their secret wars against the Germans and Japanese in World War II. Today, terrorists often use it in their symbolic wars against everyone. A police friend told me that cultists, kid gangs, and other street slime often will take a nasty dump in the office or home of some rich, powerful person after breaking into and stealing from the place. I bet you might be able to come up with ways a good bullybuster might adapt the same tactic and make it work for the good guys.

Finally, according to the Hombre of Justice, human feces mix well with chocolate or coffee ice cream and because of the freezing later involved, the odor is eliminated. This stunt gives new meaning to the order, *eat shit!*

Exotic Weapons

Did you like those exploding arrows that Sylvester Stallone used as Rambo? Want some working plans to make the same type of arrows, Claymore mines, shotgun rockets or a mortar of your own? All of these are guaranteed to work. An outfit known as Kephart Publications sells the plans and claims the finished products are cheap and easily made in your own workshop — no machine-shop tools or skills needed. Are they legal to complete and own? That's for someone else to worry about. See the *Sources* section.

Explosives

Dr. Demolition calls this explosive his 35mm Killer. Here is what you need:

1 lb. of potassium chlorate
¾ cup of 350 mesh (fine) aluminum powder
1 cup Hercules Blue Dot coarse gunpowder
$^3/_{32}$" rocket fuse
15 empty 35mm film containers
1 mortar and pestle for mixing

Here's what you do: Mix them all together using a mortar and pestle or plastic tray — anything not likely to create a spark. Also, do not allow any aluminum dust to get into the air; that stuff is dangerous.

After thoroughly mixing, use a small plastic spoon to fill the film cans. Fill fully, then tamp tightly with the ceramic pestle. Cut six inches of fuse for each bomb, prick a tiny hole in the film can lid to feed the fuse through. Before you screw on the lids, be sure you seal the threads with a super-glue. Also seal the fuse hole.

You are now ready for destruction. Dr. Demolition says that each one sounds like two M-80s going off together. Note: These are *not* waterproof, but they *are very dangerous!*

Fart

Despite the Establishment's prissy attitude to the contrary, farts are a great Hayduking device. Ask anyone who ever served in any armed forces or served time in most any nation . . . *farts 'r us,* and they can be fun. According to the more stiff-spined critics, only juveniles, fools, Uncle Gerry, Chris, the Colonel, Uncle George, myself, and a few others find farting and belching amusing. That assumption is quite incorrect. The classic literature is full of flatulence and eructation. The venerable Mark Twain devoted an entire book to the classics of farting. Farting and belching belong, so let's enjoy them.

With this in mind, I offer the following two treatises. In St. Petersburg, Florida, Joseph St. Pierre was awarded $25,000 in a lawsuit against the McDonald's hamburger chain. Among the problems St. Pierre claimed were caused by meat at McDonald's was "chronic uncontrollable gas."

"From the time I get up in the morning to the time I go to bed at night," he told the jury, "I do nothing but pass wind." St. Pierre also told the panel that friends refuse to go to dinner with him and his fellow employees "won't stand in back of him."

The *Times of India* published this item:
The daily output of flatulence from a single sheep contains enough methane gas to power a small truck for forty kilometers, according to a New Zealand scientist, reports Reuters from Wellington.
Dr. David Lowe told a conference of meteorologists that New Zealand could solve some of its fuel problems if it found a way to harness the less savory by-product of its seventy-two million sheep.

"He said the total daily methane output of New Zealand's sheep was one thousand tons. If a sheep was put on the back of a utility truck with a bale of hay and connected to the engine 'with appropriate fittings,' it could run the vehicle for about forty kilometers a day," he said.

As if these literary references to flatulence were not enough, we now learn that the conductor of the Mt. Lebanon Wind Symphony is becoming a fashion entrepreneur, announcing in all of the trade press, "This spring I will be bringing out my new line of pre-farted underwear for those willing to make such a daring fashion statement."

Singing Sam used a fart to get back at a mark through an answering machine. The mark had the usual pompous message, which Sam had a girlfriend change for him while the mark was away for a week. The new message started with someone sounding like the mark saying, "Hello, I'm out of town and want you to listen to this brief message directed personally at you before you leave your message. Here's to you. . . ." This was followed by a very loud, authentic, long and wet fart that rumbled the machine.

For further assistance see the *Sources* section.

Farting and Beyond

According to Professor Frank Snakeoil, director of Anal Athletics at Mercenary University of Propaganda (MUP), there is a perfect escalation to farting in the general direction of your mark. The next step down the evolutionary ladder is to actually take a dump — loudly and graphically — in your pants in front of the mark, his family, friends, associates, whomever. Then, take off your pants, hand them to the mark as you make a very brief speech about how appropriate the award is, turn and leave. Hopefully, a loyal colleague will have proper escape clothing and vehicle just outside for you to hasten your immediate departure.

Food

My gracious, we actually have a celebrity contributor. He plays in the backfield for a great Super Bowl team caged in Chicago. His team nickname is Sweetness and his nom de guerre for this book is Mr. Loose. It seems the Bears get on each other a lot and Mr. Loose takes his share of abuse. One day he discovered the paraffin wax that the team trainer uses for heat-treatment of injury. It has a reddish color and when melted looked just like red glaze. Mr. Loose quietly dunked some of the team's pre-game doughnuts in this wax and when it dried and hardened, the result was a glazed donut lookalike. Some taste in humor, that Mr. Loose.

In another stunt, he found that artificial fat tissue, which the trainer uses to pad the hands of the linemen, looks like cheese, although it's made of rubber. It was no problem to slip a couple of pieces into the sandwich of one of Mr. Loose's main tormentors. So much for celebrities. Now, consider this.

Whenever the gang got together, they always assumed or bullied Betty into doing the cooking. Never any thank–yous or compliments on the cooking, although it was excellent, beyond the usual patronizing waves. Betty tried all sorts of nice ways to spread the chore around. Finally, she began to put bits of cotton in the pancake batter and other additives to the various other foods. The "hints" worked and Betty soon joined the diners as someone else volunteered to cook.

Miss Illmanners handled the same basic problem by including unusual hors d'oeuvres, such as mouse paw, bunny tail, mole face, or toenail d'human, in her finger food. Same result. All of this recalls similar solutions listed in my earlier books.

Gift and gag shops are fantastic sources for the paraphernalia of Hayduking. For instance, Chris in Urbana called in on a radio talk show to tell me that he used a sheet of plastic cheese in a sandwich to get back at a food-hogging roommate. The guy ate it. I wonder if his stool resembled those little white puff-things companies use as packing?

Food Stamps

Marty and Mike have a really hip Illinois collegiate radio audience, and these folks taught me a lot of fun things to do to evil people. For example, Jeff called in to suggest that you offer in a local newspaper classified ad, "FREE FOOD STAMPS" or "DISCOUNT FOOD STAMPS — CHEAP!" and list your mark's telephone number. As a touch, you might request late-night calls due to "shift work."

After Jeff hung up, another caller volunteered the delightful idea that the feds would probably be very curious about who was giving away or selling food stamps. Gee, gang, a bonus!

Furniture Stores

Ever been had by a furniture store and been refused relief for wood that rots or splits, or upholstery that fades? The Chainsaw Queen had that happen and did something very subtle. She secreted a screwdriver on her person, and then she and a very loud, noisy, garish and sexily dressed young lady friend went to the store that was about to be in trouble.

"While my sexy friend asked questions and created the diversion, I unscrewed a whole lot of support screws out of a whole lot of furniture, especially expensive and somewhat frail pieces. Our hope was that some human tank would come in and plop down to bounce-test the strength of the furniture.

"We didn't have to wait long . . . it happened twice while we were still there. We left, holding back squalls of laughter."

Garbage

Mad Mike wrote to tell me that he got back at a crooked boss by taking my advice about the weights and measures seals on gasoline pumps. He closed that station quickly, so he did. Mike also passes along a new tip on garbaging your mark.

It works best if your mark has a large family and several garbage cans. On garbage night, wait until your mark hauls his three or four cans out to the street for morning pickup. A few hours later, when all is quiet and dark, carefully put all of his full cans back where he normally stores them. He will find them there in the morning and wonder. You can probably do this several times as the garbage piles up and up. Won't it be fun in the truly hot weather of full summer?

Gasoline

In March 1986, there was a general strike in Panama. Among other things that happened, the refineries were shut down. So pretty soon the local gas stations ran dry. The U.S. military personnel were able to gas up at the PX station, only to find out the next morning that their purchases had been siphoned off during the night.

Two U.S. Army officers from the Logistics Directorate, Major George Alexander and Chief Warrant Officer Don Maulden, experienced such losses. They understood the plight of the poor Panamanians and were genuinely concerned for their health — concerned, that is, that someone might suffer irreparable body harm as a result of improper siphoning techniques.

In the spirit of international harmony and understanding, George and Don each left a five-gallon gasoline can in his driveway that night. Each contained about four gallons of gasoline.

Each also contained five pounds of sugar.

Next morning, the cans were gone. As the officers related their experiences to our roving colleague, M. Nelson Chunder, their countenances shone with beatific radiance that can only be known by those who have unselfishly shared their possessions with others less fortunate than themselves.

Gelatin

You salacious creature, you read the contents and turned to this page first thinking of kinky things to do with gelatin mix. What I have here is much more funny, and it's from my Italian friend Andrea.

It's summer and really hot. Your mark is sleeping without pajamas, as, in the nude. You take several small packs of gelatin powder and lightly sprinkle the powder all over your mark's body, mixing little blips of one color here, another color here. Andrea, who's done this one, says body perspiration melts the powder and causes all sorts of fun colors to form on the mark's body. It will stain both body and bedding, that's for sure. Thanks, Andrea, I will think of you next time I buy gelatin.

Gossips

The rationale behind gossip is understandable if you agree with the explanation of Pauli Hayworth, one of the oustanding liberal feminists of our time. Ms. Hayworth explains, "On the evolutionary scale, Woman and the Bird are far superior to Man. That is why, of course, Man was forced to invent the telephone wire, to accommodate his two biological/intellectual superiors."

Pauli revealed how she uses the neighborhood and office gossips to help fight her wars against rude people. "It's not at all complicated. I just call the gossip and ask him or her to answer some questions I have about the mark. Of course, I don't use my own name . . . I usually pretend to be an insurance investigator or reporter.

"I ask the gossip how long Mr. Mark has been on the drug rehab program. Or, I ask if the gossip knows if Ms. Mark has been fired again for homosexuality — stuff like this," Pauli explains.

Pauli never fails to be amazed how quickly the words get around.

Graffiti

I started out using these as fillers for half empty pages, then a lot of people started sending me their favorites and on radio shows, readers called in to say they were using the graffiti from my book to make their own statements. Once more, the scrawl of the wild:

- WHEN GOD MADE MAN SHE WAS ONLY KIDDING
- IT'S A BITCH TO BE A BUTCH
- DULL WOMEN HAVE CLEAN HOMES AND MINDS
- SAVE THE BALES (pro pot message)
- I NEVER SCREW ON THE FIRST GRAM
- I COME AT NIGHT AND AM GONE BY MORNING
- THE DRUNKER I GET, THE PRETTIER YOU ARE
- TODAY, I'LL DO IT FOR LOVE, BUT TOMORROW IT'S $50
- STICKS AND STONES MAY BREAK MY BONES, BUT LEATHER REALLY EXCITES ME
- EXTRASENSORY PERVERSION — DON'T

CUM IN MY MIND
- WHAT DOES IT SAY ON THE BOTTOM OF COKE BOTTLED ON LESBOS? USE OTHER END
- TRUE AMBITION — TO BE A 50-FT WOMAN'S GYNECOLOGIST
- SOME WOMEN ARE BORN TO GREATNESS, OTHERS HAVE IT THRUST INTO THEM
- I ♠ SOIXANTE-NEUF

Gravesites

OK, enough light humor, it's back to heavy time. If you really want to shatter your mark, as in really do the sucker in, here you go. Borrow some very uninhibited friends, truck them to the gravesite of your mark's close family. Using a Polaroid camera, take pictures of your associates performing sexual and scatological acts upon the gravesite and stone.

This is a long story involving a racial bigot, some family cruelty that broke apart a young couple and their child, and, finally, the death of the bigot. The bigot's adult son was just as evil, by the way. Photos were taken showing an interracial couple doing fun things with each other on the old man's grave. Faces were not shown and the people were not local. A printed message was attached to each photo and they were disseminated to the appropriate media and local gossips:

Here is photographic proof that Elmo Hateblack is a member of the Church of Satan. He is performing Black Mass with Mistress Charlatan, high priestess, on the grave of his father, Elmer Hateblack.

Elmo is, of course, the son. Phew, this one really

made some tight sphincters in that town. Who gets credit for this messy masterpiece of black humor? Dick Smegma.

Guns

There are many new gun laws in place. Play on the ignorance of your mark and advertise him or her as a gun dealer who is selling guns which are now classed as illegal. List fairly cheap prices, but, don't be too unrealistic. List the mark's address and phone number. Always remember to include the magic phrase, "I've discovered a *big* loophole in the federal gun laws." That line insures *strong* government interest in your mark.

If you have a mark who's an obnoxiously anti-gun person, you might wish to do one of two things. (1) If you have the money, make a hefty cash contribution in his or her name to the Citizens Committee For The Right To Keep And Bear Arms. Or, (2), you may wish to make a hefty pledge in the mark's name. I would accompany this donation/pledge with letters to the editors of your local newspapers and one or more of the gun publications. For addresses, see the Useful Addresses section of this book.

Actually, this is a success story, but I wasn't sure if I ought to place it there, or in the humor section. I decided to call a fool by its own name, and so placed it here. Enjoy, as the contributor, Von Henry, is a good guy, and, as the Rev. Paul Wilson once wrote, "Guns . . . you're only caught dead without one."

Von Henry relates how someone he knew wished to get back at a person who was the head of his state's version of the Anti-Handgun Gang. He needed to get back at him for another reason, but used this affiliation to wipe out his mark. This may be a useful object lesson.

Von says his pal wrote a batch of letters to various people and groups using the mark's name and letterhead. The first batch went to groups like Handgun Control, Inc., and informed them that he had seen the truth now about gun control and it was the work of the devil, the International Communist Conspiracy and was related to the spread of AIDS, child molestation, unions, and democrats.

Next, he "had" Mr. Mark write to groups like the NRA, CCRTKBA, and others pledging undying support and enclosing small cash contributions. He requested literature, membership information, and info on how to form a local fund-raising group.

The third batch of mail to go out under Mr. Mark's name went to both state and federal officials, legislators and congressmen, demanding a repeal of the Gun Control Act of 1968. In this letter he also threatened to raise funds and to work to defeat any "communist-loving, sonofabitch traitor" who opposed his views.

Finally, Mr. Mark "sent" letters to a variety of newspapers in the state accusing nearly everyone in that state, except himself, of being a communist/fascist/homosexual/democrat. He managed to make the KKK seem like a Desmond Tutu fan club, he was so rabid. Horrendously, many newspapers print letters without checking and in this case, it happened.

I am pausing now only to let your imagination try to cope with the fallout this campaign caused in terms of legal, moral, personal, political and paranoid confusion, and quandry. My salute goes out to Von Henry and his friend for a job well done.

Hangovers

Don Wildmon is one of those friends with whom you don't want to go out overdrinking. He has a massively creative sense of evil. His favorite is when someone has a world class hangover, i.e., the kind that makes you wish you were the poster child for immediate terminal illness.

"You find the worst, most horrible rubber monster mask possible at a costume shop and hold it until this moment of submental hangover melange, when the mark is tossing between the line of malt madness and mindless malaise . . . and decides to take a shower," Don says.

"The next move is to make it to the shower before your mark and install the mask over the shower head so that the water will pour out semi-normally through the eyes, nose and mouth of the mask. Then, you unscrew the lightbulb in the shower room so the area is in semi-darkness.

"The mark will stumble in and manage to adjust the water . . . all drunks have that guidance ability. As soon as some degree of new wakening is witnessed by you — hiding in the shadows — HIT THE LIGHTS!"

The result is usually physical freakout of a level achieved by Jason Vorhees while he terrorizes third grade girls seeing their first *Friday the 13th* movie on the VCR while mom and dad are out for the evening. The effect is embellished, by the way, if you can somehow introduce red dye to the water flow.

Help Lines

I thank Ray from Kansas City for sharing this scary, but very effective, stunt. I will change some of the details to protect the source, but in essence, here's how it happened.

A man was in the process of a nasty divorce and was living alone in an apartment. About 11:30, a police tactical squad burst into his room, subdued this terrified guy, slapped a strait jacket on him, and hustled him off to a psychiatric hospital. He was almost hysterical, which added to the effectiveness of the situation.

He was shot with drugs, after having had his stomach pumped, then strapped into a bed for observation. After an hour he was told that *he* had called the Human Suicide Rescue Hotline and reported that he'd taken poison and, further, was going to blow up the neighborhood with a TNT bomb in his apartment, or shoot any police who came looking for him.

It took him another hour, plus several confirming telephone calls, to get across that this was a hoax. He was released with very little apology. In fact, they were angry at him for being "the kind of person in his situation who would get taken advantage of and make fools of the authorities.'' No apology — get out. He found his apartment had been tossed and torn by the police bomb squad, plus his landlady was evicting him on the spot because of the incident.

The guy figured his estranged wife had somehow engineered the entire thing. She, of course, was out of state with tight alibis and acted insulted, threatening to sue him if he dragged her into the thing.

Wow . . . that's heavy duty! But, if anyone can use it, you have K.C. Ray's blessing.

Highways

Kepler McGeary, one of the Wild Bunch from Idaho, decided one day to tie up traffic badly on his least favorite freeway to his least favorite city. He borrowed a heavy dump truck full of municipal gravel while a friend drove another. Together, they headed to the pre-chosen bottleneck spot far between exit ramps, as they had planned the event well in advance after much thought, checking of alternative routes, maps, and potential rescue efforts by authorities. Says Kepler:

"We reached the spot and swung our rigs head to head, blocking three of the four lanes. We already had a long line of cars behind us — we started out just as morning rush hour did. We quickly dumped our loads of gravel which totally jammed the entire parkway. We both quickly left the cabs of the trucks, and with a valve buster let the air out of tires on both vehicles. We then fled to the next ramp where a colleague picked us up."

"Nobody saw us escape and there were no clues as to what happened. We got away with it and blocked traffic for four hours that morning. Made TV, too. I think the city fathers knew what had happened but didn't want the public to know."

Hit 'n Run Drivers

Some brainless driver once struck the car of Major General K. Oss and immediately chose to become a hit 'n run statistic. Unwise, as the general witnessed the event and obtained the license number of the foolish one. He easily traced it using techniques from a book that personal modesty forbids me to mention here. Here's the drill after you find the guilty party.

"With a bit of effort you can remove the hinge pins on your mark's car door, as I did," the general explained. "The door is then carefully reshut for the mark to open and spill to the ground. Or, it may hold, hopefully, even after the mark's reshutting. The door will then fall off when the mark takes the next corner. Perhaps, the mark will not be wearing a seat belt and will join the door in the roadway."

Horns

It's dangerous, silly, risky, but funny. Mr. Death says if you want to keep your mark awake at night or otherwise harass him during the evening hours, horn in on his time. Our Australian friend says to buy cheap bicycle horns that use batteries to make their awful sound. Buy a dozen of them. Hide them in and around your mark's home, office and/or apartment. Run around and insert batteries into each and keep on moving . . . quickly.

Another way to drive a mark horny is to put a cheap timer device on his car horn, so that it will be set off ablaring at 4 or 5 in the old A.M. This is a nice way to get back at someone you know who tailgates and is always quick on the horn trigger for other drivers.

Impersonations

Vaughn Meador and Rich Little have inspired a lot of Haydukery. For example, one of my old pals, who was a radio reporter in the early '60s, used to call his buddies at the *New York Times* and *Washington Post* whenever a nasty story about JFK would appear. He sounded more like JFK than the President. Anyway, pretending to be JFK, my pal would lambaste the newspaper guys, then start to get personal about their wives and girlfriends. It made for fun. Is there a lesson in there for you? I hope so.

Speaking of JFK, the men who conspired to have him murdered in Dallas also used impersonation to make a patsy out of an innocent dupe named Lee Harvey Oswald. They used at least one, maybe two, Oswald look-alikes to do bizarre things in that area so people would remember the man and the name. Is there a lesson in there for you? I hope so.

Impersonate your mark or hire someone to impersonate the mark. Do awful, rotten things in the mark's name. In addition to the people who killed John Kennedy, this stunt is a favorite trick of such fun folks as those at the CIA and the KGB.

Incinerators

If your rotten landlord's place or your least favorite school has a master trash incinerator, it is fun to dump empty aerosol cans into the chutes and listen to the explosive fun that follows about ten seconds later. Don't use cans full of paint, though, or you get a very dramatic pyrotechnical effect when they explode, as in major firebomb time.

A caller from Cleveland had such a tough time getting her landlord to clean up apartments as he ignored her completely. She went to a dozen barber shops and collected a lot of human hair, as in two garbage bags full. Have you ever smelled human hair burning? If not, take my word for it, hair smells worse than a whole body barbeque. Anyway, my caller from Cleveland dumped all of this collected human hair into the incinerator of her building. Within three hours, state and federal agencies had the landlord under close investigation.

Interoffice Memos

If you've ever been in an interoffice political war you know the destructive power of memo missiles. Our Jimmy Carter, as opposed to Georgia's Mr. Peanut, adds to your office arsenal with a forgotten weapon — the envelope. Jimmy writes, "As most of these interoffice envelopes are frequently reused by crossing off the last name before readdressing it, you can use this fact to create paranoia or to spread blame for a nasty and/or anonymous memo to some secondary mark."

Simply send a nasty, filthy, gross or totally insulting memo to your mark, but use the envelope listing the previous address of another mark. The mark adds two and two and comes up with a major error.

Intestines

Kansas City's Ray had an uncaring neighbor who used to toss garbage into Ray's yard. Bad form. Ray tossed it back after trying to reason with the neighbor. No luck, the guy just didn't care and kept dumping. Ray has this friend who works at a meat slaughtering and packing plant across the river, over in Missouri. Ah heck, let's let Ray finish his story. "So, we picked up two barrels of guts from the plant, and that night we spread them on the neighbor's porch. You gotta know just how hot it is in Kansas City in the deep summer. I don't know which was worse, the flies or the stink."

Was Ray bothered again?

"The guy called the police, but, hey, I was at work, and had a great alibi. In fact, I really sympathized with the guy, pretended while the cops were there that I was a great buddy and caring neighbor who was really upset with this awful deed. What a blast. He quit bugging me. No more garbage in my yard."

IRS

Tax reform. Remember that rich folk rip-off that went through Congress like a dose of salts in 1986? True tax reform, honesty that would help you and me instead of the rich folks who buy this country's politicians and lawmakers, is about as likely as William Perry getting a job as a jockey. Left with that, let's use what we have.

Office supply stores sell Taxpayer File Systems, a filing system for your papers, bills, receipts, and checks. It's your own file-stop center for all of your income-tax related papers. Buy one of these and create a file for your mark. Put in a bunch of miscellaneous papers, receipts, dubious claims, and weakly documented deductions. Make it a mess. Make it look like fraud. Make it insulting. Then, around April 10, bundle up the whole thing and send it to the IRS with a cover letter. This letter should be smug, insulting, and cocky. Tell them to figure out the deductions. Include a very sloppy 1040 return for your mark with lots of obviously weak and illegal deductions. Insult the IRS. Caution: Remember my rules when doing something like this as you're dealing with a *very heavy* federal outfit. Be cool and cautious. But, have fun!

Jocks

At last, an up-to-date athlete who has something new to stuff in your mark's jockstrap — Nair. According to Todd from Phoenix, sweat really does the trick, activating the ingredients which turn your mark back to his prepubescence. Hair today, gone today, is Todd's motto.

Another jocularity comes from athletic supporter Jock Worthen, who gets off on nasty photos. The idea here is to use copied photos of jock or underwear ads with normal models. Or, you can take your own photos with grossly fat models, female models, or whatever. The next step is to composite your mark's head/facial photo on the body of whatever or whomever you've chosen to wear the jock. Whatever way, your mark loses, especially if the photo gains exceptionally wide circulation, like at grade schools and junior and senior high schools with appropriate warnings. I like that portrait, do you?

Junque Mail

After the last book, I got a very uptight-assed letter from the Direct Mail Marketing Association complaining about the nasty things I had written about "direct mail" (aka junk mail), and explaining how vital this commercial mail is to the American economy, how much it means to the lives of the elderly and shut-ins. In this book I vow to dress up my style somewhat. Thus, I will no longer use the term junk mail. It is now as you see it above, junque mail.

Schizoid Sam has come up with a different way to deal with the creative cretins who fill your mailbox with their ploys to transfer funds from your pocket to theirs. He writes, "I always respond to their requests for my financial support to aid their questionable causes. I check the highest amount requested and send them either Monopoly money or one of those 'Dear Name, you may have already won $1,000,000' bogus checks that other junk mailers send out. I figure this is fun, insults them, and I add $$ injury to that by using their postpaid envelopes to return my nastiness in."

Jury Duty

Nobody has caught up with him yet, but authorities in one Pennsylvania county are looking for a man who had called six women and, posing as a court official, ordered them to report for "emergency jury duty" at the courthouse at 5 a.m. the next day. He told them they would be fined if they did not appear. Each did so. The friend who sent me the newspaper clippings about the incident said that authorities were looking for a possible co-worker or neighbor, which sounds to me like they have nothing to go on. It's a cute scam for all involved.

Landlords

A thoughtful gift for an errant landlord comes from the Lord God of Vengeance, who says an ant farm makes a fine going-away present, especially if it's left in some obscure location where only a dedicated and/or expensive exterminator can find it.

Another friendly fan, an old, toss-back hippie named Joe Donolay, is truly a relic from another era. But, he has a message for nasty landlords who do mean things to innocent tenants. Joe suggests that you "call the landlord's mother if there are gross, disgusting sex 'n drug parties in your building. Invite her to the party and tell her that her son is the prime sponsor . . . hey, he owns the building. Naturally, you don't tell her in advance what kind of party she's getting involved with."

Joe says this has worked well for him three or four times.

Law Enforcement

Sometimes people who give assholes a bad name get into the law-enforcement business, a growth industry that has more than its share of hypocrites. Perhaps you have real, honest reason to get back at a cop, sheriff, district attorney, constable, or whatever. Here is one way to doing it, thanks to my inside source, Edwin Mouse.

According to Edwin, many of these hypocrites break more laws than they enforce and are living proof that there are at least two or three systems of justice in our world. One of their universal traits is that they like to party.

"I recall one time when there was a truly hated man serving as DA, sheriff, chief, or whatever, and a lot of people had it in for him for really good reasons. These were not crooks or slimes bitter about being caught. These were straight people with legit gripes about this arrogant jackass. Here is what someone did," Edwin told me.

"The guy had a big party with lots of booze and food. A lot of his criminal justice buddies and their women showed up, of course. And, like most of these bashes, a lot of people got really tuned up. Our trickster had told some news people to crash the party quietly 'for a scoop.' Our trickster also made certain that 'someone' had stashed a goodly amount of coke in the house.

"Then, 'someone' made certain that some of the tuned folks who might like coke ('someone' really did homework) got into the stash, in a room where the host had no idea what was happening. About three minutes later, some on-duty officers who were straight and honest and had been quietly tipped about this whole operation by 'someone' came to the door and were easily admitted. They went right to the coke room, as did the news people."

The rest of the story is a study in confusion, embarrassment, news frenzy, political gossip, sexual gossip, and a lot of real ethical questions. The majority of the mark's political mentors — older men not at the party — took a very, very dim view of the entire situation, regardless of what was said in the mark's defense.

Actually, as Edwin Mouse told me, there was more damage done to the mark by what was not published or prosecuted than by what was made public. See, there really is justice, if you're willing to go out and get it for yourself.

Lawns

Our intrepid landscape demolisher, Mr. Heffer
from Missouri, had a nasty, nosy neighbor who used to
scold Mr. Heffer for not taking care of his lawn like the
neighbor did her prized lawn. Mr. Heffer decided to attract more attention for her lawn.

"I waited until June, when the local K-Mart was
selling garden plant seeds for about a nickel a bag and I
bought all of their leaf lettuce seeds . . . I went over to
that old biddy's lawn and tossed those seeds all over the
place one night when we were due to get a day or two of
rain. No need to scratch that stuff in . . . just toss it
amid the grass. It grows great and soon she had the
damnedest-looking lawn you ever saw."

Added to that idea, The Lord God of Vengeance
says that he uses either clover or dandelion seeds to get
the same effect from a crabby, bluegrass freak who
refuses to have any impure strains in his putter-perfect
lawn.

When Bill Murray played Karl, the gifted assistant
greenskeeper in that wonderful film *Caddyshack,* I
knew genius had arrived. If ever there is a Hayduke
movie, we gotta get that Karl character in there. Darren

from Arizona isn't the same character, but, he has a wonderful landscape suggestion if your mark loves his lawn as much as Ted Knight loved his golf greens in *Caddyshack*.

Darren says, "You pour lots of liquid Dawn detergent all over the mark's lawn. When it rains or is watered, it bubbles all over the place, like green champagne."

Several readers have asked me for less esoteric and expensive weed-killers to use in having fun with marks' lawns. Try this: Mix one part laundry bleach with three or four parts of water. Sprinkle it at random on plants or lawn, use it to make fun designs, or to write funny and/or foul words.

Leprosy

I became interested in this disease many years ago when Lenny Bruce was masquerading as a Catholic priest and hustling rich, guilt-ridden Jewish folks in Miami to contribute to a leper colony he had founded. It was very quasi-legal even if he did get busted. Later, when Jerry Lewis passed over leprosy, hangnails, and psoriasis, settling on Jerry's Kids as his telethon disease, I knew the day of our truth would come.

That day hasn't come yet. But, in the meantime, you could go to your favorite printer and create some letterhead from a law firm or some state government agency that would be hard to trace. On this letterhead you could create a letter to be sent to all folks in the neighborhood, condo, apartment complex, or whatever saying that Mr. or Ms. Mark, the owner, is selling the property for use as a leprosarium. You may embellish the remainder of the letter, then imagine the response.

Letters

Despite the frothy-mouthed ravings of the old pharts who run the Reaganista Party, the Soviets do have a sense of humor. There is an old Soviet practice known as *anonimka,* in which someone writes an anonymous letter to a superior or party official falsely accusing a colleague of misconduct at the office, factory, school, or institute. Soviet officials are, believe it or not, far more paranoid than Reaganistas, although we are closing the frump gap quickly, and tend to overreact in the zeal to investigate.

Anonimka has created more than one major flap in the Party and among what passes for industry in the USSR. Recently, *Izvestia* editorialized against the practice, tirading against "false, cowardly attacks." The Soviet press tries to discourage people from using anonimka to get back at their enemies by slandering them.

I checked with my publisher and so far we haven't sold the Soviet Union rights to my books, so they can't blame anonimka on me. Otherwise, it's a pretty doggone good stunt. It was Sir Edward Bulwer-Lytton who said, "The pen is mightier than the sword," but as I'll add, that's only if you're willing to push it.

Machismo

A lot of guys think with their zippers, which soon becomes a pain in the ego to normal people. That very splendid lady, Paulette Cooper, has a fun idea to get a mite of revenge. She uses a picture of a gorgeous lady and a handwritten note about how wonderful she heard the mark is in bed, and how very good she is, and that they ought to get together. She leaves a telephone number. That's the kicker.

"You use one of your local telephone company's line test numbers because it's always busy — the phone that rings forever," Paulette says.

She suggests a variant where you've actually been out with the mark. Here you get a photo of some beautiful lady who looks like you — never use your own photo. It's okay to be romantically explicit in the note, by the way. Either way, the guy ends up frustrated, physically or mentally.

Mafia

Every so often the feds or state police bust a Mafia chieftain, sometimes on pretty serious charges. You can use this criminal to aid your cause. As anyone who knows the Crime Corporation's operations will tell you, these powerful bosses retain their control even while in the slam. Thus, it would be fun if your mark wrote a vile, nasty, threatening, mocking, or other not-nice letter to this Mob boss. You could include some "doing the dozens" about the guy's family, his parish priest, his momma, too.

Shortly after this letter is received I bet your mark will be visited by some large gentlemen who don't have necks. What happens next is of amusement to you, no doubt.

Dick Smegma adds some refinement to my basic idea by noting that you should send a copy of the letter to the guy's attorney. He also cautions that you wear gloves to type the letter, use a typewriter other than your own, use totally sanitized paper, and wet the stamp with a sponge and not your tongue. If the Mob guy is from another city, either have the letter mailed from there or from the mark's own town.

Mail

Mr. Death is both funny and useful. He suggests you simply steal your mark's rural letterbox in the evening. The postal people will obviously not deliver mail if there is no rural box. Mr. Death says that the mark will put up a new one. You wait a day and then steal it. Do this several times, after you are sure the mark and/or the postal inspectors are not looking for you. Here's the kicker: after a year or so has passed, drive by the mark's place and toss out all of the purloined postal boxes onto his lawn.

Or, if your mark lives in an unincorporated suburb, township or rural area, the mail comes to a large, post-mounted mailbox. You could change the name and/or number of your mark's box. This will confuse the carrier for a day or two, which may be enough to pull a short scam.

I love cooked eggs, dripping with butter, a great habit I picked up in Mexico. I later learned from Major General K. Oss that he loves cooked eggs also, but, in this case, the yoke is on the mark. The general says that lightly cracked eggs placed in your mark's mailbox on a hot summer's day quickly cook into a very odorous mess. Perhaps if they are placed there after the mail service on Saturday, they will have all day Sunday to strengthen.

I checked this out with my postal consultant, Paco Pendeja, who told me that the postal carrier is likely to be as upset by this mess as the mark himself. Also, the carrier is in a position to add further to the mark's woes about the mess, according to Paco.

Mail Forwarding

I get a lot of requests for outfits that do mail forwarding. To find them, scan the classifieds in such magazines as *Rolling Stone, Mother Jones,* and *Moneysworth,* or look through some of the counter-culture publications. But, because mail forwarding and drop boxes are always so important to Haydukers, I am listing some here which are very professional in operation. If you have others which you've used and wish to add to my list, please let me know.

- **Abell**
  520 Isabel Dr.
  Santa Cruz, CA 95060

- Mail Forwarding
  Box 125
  Wynnewood, PA 19096

- Morris & Morris
  P.O. Box 80767
  Los Angeles, CA 90008

- Zebra Mail Center
  P.O. Box 11028
  Houston, TX 77391

Magazines

You'll have to wait until the statute of limitations expires before I identify the magazine in question here, but, let me tell you how I got nasty with one that had rudely and crudely allowed its computers to do me in. I won't bore you with details, but it managed to screw up my initial subscription, extension of same, and an address change. All of this within two years, and I was eventually getting dunned by a collection agency on three separate bills for which I was getting no magazines. It cost me a $20 trip to small claims court to get them off my back and the matter settled. *Phew!*

Here's what I did next. By this time, I also had five other people to whom I owed some hassle of varying degrees. I got a new subscriber card for each mark to this, my least favorite magazine. No, it's not funny nor especially clever, but I know it cost my main magazine mark some serious money and I know it cost my other marks some time, energy, and letter hassle.

As I've said before, to be effective, you don't always have to be clever or funny.

On the other hand, there is Schizoid Sam who knows a way to obtain magazines more inexpensively than you are now, unless you're stealing them. He points out, quite correctly, that college student rates are the absolute lowest in the business, the idea being to hook those potential consumers early. Sam suggests you become a "student" to take advantage of these low subscription rates. Here's how.

"Go to the bookstore at the nearest college or university and pick up those subscription fliers that are on counters, bulletin boards, etc. You an also find them in all classrooms, as companies pay kids to post them.

"These fliers list hundreds and hundreds of magazines at special student rates. You simply fill out your name and address, and send them a check for whatever you want. They will ask you for your year of graduation . . . so let's make you a junior. That means you write in next year's date there. When you renew or subscribe again, just add a year. So many of these come in to them each year that nobody checks anyway," Sam relates.

By now, everyone knows how to order thousands of magazines for hundreds of marks or how to get your own subscriptions more cheaply. Here's a new twist from the Idaho Wildman, who says you can order a select few magazines especially chosen to hit the mark where it hurts hardest. For example, he says, "Suppose your mark is some evil woman whose husband escaped by running off with a nurse. Subscribe to a few nursing journals in her name, using a gift card to Bitch, from The Happy Couple." The neat thing about this is every hobby and every occupation has at least one special interest journal or magazine of its own.

Meat Shoppes

I love custom butcher shops, always have. I've never been to a bad one. But, Macho has, and he really beat their meat in response. He got a bad steak — tough. He returned the unused portion and was told to "forget it" when asking for some adjustment.

"I was really reasonable about it, too," Macho says. "I showed the guy the meat and my receipt. He said I bought some cheap beef somewhere else, pulled a switch, and was trying to cheat him. We argued and argued; then he threatened to call the cops. I left. But had he screwed up!"

Macho knew of a real putz who also shopped there, a guy he wanted to nail for another reason. It looked like combined revenge time. Macho called the market in the other mark's name and ordered over a hundred dollars' worth of fine meat. He adds, "Don't go whole hog and run up a big bill. Keep it believable."

He had a girlfriend from outside the neighborhood pick up the other mark's order and charge it to that mark's account. Macho says, "Man, we ate well for a long time on that scam. It never would have happened if old Mr. Butcher hadn't been dishonest with me."

Media

I despise the misuse of this word in reference to people who work for magazines, newspapers, radio, and television because it is almost always used incorrectly, plus it has become a buzz word.

Here's your language lesson. Media is the plural form of medium. Radio, for example, is a medium. Radio, newspapers, TV, etc. are media. They are mass communication media. Reporters, commentators, writers, journalists, and anchortwinkies are *not* media. They are people who work for media, even if many of them don't know the difference. Now, here's the rest of it.

This section is devoted to Joey Skaggs, a very well-known scam artist who preys on "Media" much like the roadrunner destroys Wile E. Coyote. In my opinion, he has proved himself worth his weight in disloyalty to the system and in showing how easily it is manipulated.

Skaggs' forte is to plant phony stories and appear on interviews to spread sillymation. Some of his classics that made ocean-to-ocean news across the U.S. included sperm banks for the stars (celebrities), a bordello for dogs, fish condos, etc. He's been at it since 1966. Even in the summer of 1986, he nailed *Good Morning America* with his Fat Squad, in which he claimed dieters hired strong people to physically restrain them from eating. No, I'm not kidding. Ask the very embarrassed David Hartman, GMA's host.

An artist and visual arts professor in New York City, Skaggs has used his own name and pen names, and has appeared under different funny names for more than twenty years now. He has fooled the Establishment media, and his scams have appeared in all major newspapers, wire services, and networks. Sometimes he gets calls *weeks* after his hoaxes are broken. Some of his other stories include:

- A coalition of ethnic descendants going to court to protest the name "gypsy" in gypsy moth.
- Development of cockroach hormones into a medicine that cures acne and menstrual cramps.
- "Crazed" U.S. Special Forces detachment "attacked" a Nativity scene in New York's Central Park (he partially staged this).

Why does all of this work? Mostly because a lot of news people are lazy, and a lot more are gullible, and many just "want to believe" so they can share it with the public. Finally, don't ever forget the most widely read newspaper in America is *National Enquirer* and remember that more Americans read *TV Guide* than any other publication. I rest my case.

Medical

I'm not sure if this is for or against us, but one doctor in every fifty is operating with bogus credentials, according to a 1985 study by a U.S. Congressional subcommittee on national health care. Perhaps a study is in order to see which group gives the better care: 49 of 50, or 1 of 50. In any case, if you should happen to find out, please let me know. I am always happy to get stories of and from the medical industry for the next book.

For this volume, the only funny medical story I heard was from The Intestine Internist who says that someone got really upset at a local doctor in the Boston area who spent more time on the golf course than on his practice or family.

On one rare night when Dr. Mark had to stay at one of the hospitals in that city, his unhappy assailant used some 2 by 4 boards to build forms around the back tires of the Doc's Porsche. He then poured a bit of premixed, quick-dry cement into the forms. Within the hour, the doctor's $52,000 auto and, I guess, its owner, were sentenced to the area for awhile. Some guys get away with mortar!

Mercenary

Given the mood of the middle-mind American mentality, this one will work well. It feeds on the Soldier of Glory image that too many Ameridiots adopt. The basic idea is as simple as the marks: you buy an ad in one of the *Soldier of Fantasy* glossy-color comic books that run Mercwork ads, using your mark's name. Be sure to include real heavy active duty service in Vietnam, the Middle East, or Central America, and that the mark's Military Occupational Speciality (MOS) is one of the combat/intelligence number groups.

What's the scam? Various elements of the U.S. government are not happy about private soldiers making and carrying out deadly foreign policy. Thus, *big* trouble with the U.S. authorities can come to your unsuspecting mark. In addition, in the past few years there have been some rather well-publicized cases in which "mercenaries" have been recruited from such ads to do some highly illegal things, e.g., bust dopers out of prison, murder spouses, smuggle explosives to some Middle East baddies.

Military

Going from merc to military is often no more than a jump out of the old sheepdip pen. Anyway, when Lt.C. Mac was a lot younger, he spent some time in Vietnam. He once had a rare chance to get a bit of R 'n' R, but had to get bumped on a very brass-crowded flight. As a junior officer at the time, he had little chance to be on that flight until he met the flight manifest sergeant with the Circle F Brand.

"I was dumbfounded when this smiling NCO told me I had made the flight; he'd gotten me aboard," Lt.C. Mac recalls. "He told me he had bumped some people because of official priorities. Nobody questioned it; there was a war on. But, I was hardly official. I must have looked like a lost dummy, so he explained it to me."

The flight manifest sergeant told our hero, "Well, sir, your driver sergeant told me you are an OK man and a good officer. That counts for you. Now, sir, look on this flight list. See some of these names with a little 'F' penciled next to them? That little 'F' is our code to fuck over those people because they deserve it."

Lt.C. Mac stared, then said, "What about the big

135

'F' with the circle around it?''

"Well sir, that means to *really* fuck that guy over, like bump him, yet send his luggage to Alaska or have a crewman dump it overboard, or to lose his papers at the other end if we don't bump him. We have quite an unofficial officer evaluation network, sir.''

The point of Lt.C. Mac's nice little story is that if you or a friend are in a position to put circled 'F' marks next to people's names on passenger or other duty lists, please keep that power in mind. Also, this stunt will work well when you leave the military and are reborn a civilian. It also can tell you something about the *real* Golden Rule.

I got this next idea after reading some really horrifying letters a former GI in Vietnam wrote to his pal just before he deserted and went over to the other side. A friend of mind, an investigative reporter who did an article on "Turncoats in Action for the VC," based much of his work on government documents and intelligence reports about these Americans who not only deserted, but also took up arms against their countrymen. The notes, copies of reports, letters, and his story gave me this idea.

You write a very subversive letter from your mark to one of that mark's best friends, a sweetheart, a family member, a hometown newspaper editor, the unit chaplain, a former teacher, coach, or whatever. You really fill it with a lot of anti-American, pro-Commie stuff. Make it really radical and theme it so it reads like the mark is about to go over and/or do serious damage to (sound of bugles) *National Security*.

Also make certain that a rough draft or other copy of this letter is left lying around an office, dayroom, barracks, rec center, or somewhere that a *right*-thinking GI troop will find it. By now, I am sure you have guessed the rest.

Considering the normal paranoia of the military and adding on today's super-heated anti-Communist propaganda, your mark is going to be in a whole lot of trouble, even if he eventually beats this rap. The term "military justice" is just as nonsensical a contradiction as "military intelligence," but with a much longer arm and memory.

When my demented mind flashes back to those fun 'n gory days, I always trip over George Orwell's famous quote which is lying around with my mental blocks: "Those who take the sword perish by the sword. Those who don't take the sword perish by smelly diseases."

Orwell was a military man; also British, you know.

Milk Carton Kids

I learned about one of the nastier pieces of sabotage during a telephone talk show in New Orleans, when a delightful chap told how he used the media-creation hysteria of "missing kids" to do in his mark. I refer to the missing kids thing as Milk Carton Kids, but, please, don't get me wrong, I love milk. Anyway, here's his scam.

"I created a missing kid with the help of a printer and a friend who was a retired cop and also hated this mark of ours. We created just enough cover to make the kid seem real to someone with more than casual interest.

"Then we created a small investigation and carefully created enough media interest to get some modest coverage. After a week or so, we created 'witnesses' who had seen the abduction, all in the form of another public announcement. We circulated a description and 'police artist' sketch.

"Guess who the description and sketch, which we had an artist friend do from a picture, looked like? Right you are — our mark. Our next step was to have these run off and posted all over town. It wasn't long until real police interest was generated, which brought

138

heavier media attention.

"The guy got really hyper and denied everything, in a panic. You know, the 'Oh God, yes, I quit beating my wife' kind of thing. Eventually, he was cleared, but it took much more expense and energy on his part than it did on the police's part. They just dropped the thing, after giving him hell for looking like the suspect and acting guilty."

Molesters

Serious child molestation is far too serious for Hayduking. It calls for radical surgery, e.g., meatball circumcision with a rusted chain saw. But, as Dick Smegma points out, the concept of molestation may be used as the basis of a revenge stunt against some deserved jerk. It works like this. Acting as an outraged parent, you write a nasty letter to the mark in which you imply that he or she has molested your child. The trick is not to make direct accusation, but to rely on innuendo and the ability of neighbors' imaginations to fill in the worst. Copies of the letter are sent to all of the neighbors, coworkers or whomever, as well as local law-enforcement people, child welfare officials, etc.

A sample of Dick's letter follows:

Mr. Mark Nasty
1234 5th Street
Anytown, USA

Dear Mr. Nasty:

This is to inform you that, in the future, you will refrain from approaching and/or addressing my eight-year-old daughter.

You will *not* touch her in any way, shape, or form.

You will *not* refer to her as "Honey," "Darling," "Sugar Pie," "Sweetie," "Baby-doll," "Baby-Cakes," "Sugar Lips," or "Lovey-Poo."

You will *not* offer her any candy or gifts of jewelry, regardless of the time of year, or her own birthday.

You will *not* offer her transportation in any vehicle for any reason, whatsoever.

In short, you are to stay ten (10) feet away from my daughter at all times.

A copy of this letter is being simultaneously sent to every resident of your apartment building, and every resident within 1,000 feet of your apartment building, plus the Chief of Police, and the Office of the District Attorney.

If *any* of the above prohibitions is perpetrated by you against my daughter, appropriate criminal and civil legal action against you will follow.

Sincerely,

The Mother of a Terrified Little Girl

Motels

Larry is a businessman who must travel. When budgets are tight, he stays in smaller motels not quite as ostentatious as the deluxe, gilt-rated places or the Holiday Clone-American Inns. He usually gets clean lodgings. But, not always . . .

"It was kind of late. I had to get off the road to prepare for a sales presentation in the morning. The place was horrible. The maid from Motel Hell haunted me there. The service was horrible and my bed buddies had four legs and crawled. Yuk," Larry said with a shudder.

When he complained in the morning, both the clerk and the maid gave *him* verbal hell — turned out they were married (brother and sister, I'd bet). Anyway, Larry had a pal who sold medical supplies, and he saw him before going back there.

"It took some doing and a couple of bucks, but I was able to get an old lab cadaver. 'We' checked in with me using a fake name and ID. I had my 'friend' in the car. But, I brought him in the room, put the stiff in bed, and with a show of going out on the town, left — never to return."

Larry said he often wondered about the maid's reaction when she found the cadaver the next morning. "I wonder if she thought she'd crawl in with him and get a little action — they were pretty evenly matched. Or, maybe she just ate him. She was quite a ghoul; that place sure was old Motel Hell."

In another instance, Larry checked into a much more expensive motel and found dirt, cigarette stubs, and other evidence of the previous guests — the room had been dusted by a wisk, whisper, and promise but, never cleaned. Again, his complaint to the night clerk brought a bored yawn as the guy barely looked up from his paperback. He assigned Larry another room.

The next morning, Larry waited until the maid had made up the room, and did a good job. He left just as she did. He carefully did not lock the door as he closed it.

"I checked out, handed in the key, left the building, and then quickly doubled up the back stairs, entered the room, and carefully slipped that sanitary seal band from the toilet cover. I next had a very pleasing and full-morning sit-down, shut the lid, replaced the band, locked the room, and left the area."

Did you notice in there anywhere that Larry said he flushed the thing? Hmm, neither did I.

Neighbors

Thanks to Chris Schaefer's diligent reporting, we know of a wonderful success story in which Mike Waldrop of Oak Grove, Oregon, got even with a land rapist who ruined Mike's lovely view by building an ugly multi-story building butted against Mike's property. As usual, the coven of big $$$ attorneys had everything greased against him, so Mike had only one way to get even.

He painted the back of his house in multi-colored checkered patterns, put bright red wavy lines on his roof, then painted a seven-foot mural of a chunky man exposing his posterior toward the new building. Mike cast the old "moonglow" at the land rapist. Thanks, too, Chris, for sharing this with us.

Because Margaret Mead had died and she didn't know to whom else to turn, Sandy in Châteauguay reported to me that the Missing Link and his brood were living next to her in that quaint village in Quebec.

"I can't speak to them, as all they do is grunt and root. Their horrible offspring come into my yard and frighten my animals and plants. I fear they may try to copulate with my animals. They stand outside my house to watch me eat meals. The adults from this den next door throw trash into my yard and wander around filthy and frightening. You, George, gave me the inspiration to rise above the usual banal attempts with police, animal control officers, public welfare officials, etc."

What the wonderful Sandy conjured up involved the use of journalists, always a wonderful secondary mark because of their blind junkie's need for a fix of the sensational and bizarre. She came up with ideas to "tip" reporters to a great story involving the Bumpus Neighbors and their address:

- A crazy cult holed up there with guns and hostages.
- A terrorist cell planning to recapture Quebec for the Queen.
- A home robbery in progress.
- A teenage prostitution center.

I'm sure you get the idea. A little bit of scam, a bit of paranoia, some quarters dropped on those neighbors to the press and police and an instant "situation" is created — never mind the made-up stuff from Sandy.

Did she do it? Is the fact that Sandy moved just before the "event" went down any indication? Did it work? Would you be reading it here if it hadn't?

Divorce doesn't have to be all bad, or, as Mr. Justice points out, it doesn't even have to happen. He likes to run an ad in a local newspaper saying something like: "Moving out of town (or to small apartment) due to divorce. Free patio and lawn furniture, yours for hauling away." Mr. Justice says to do this when the mark is away for the day or weekend. But, why wait? It could be just as much fun to have the mark there to deal with the problem, considering how rude human vultures can be when they think they're getting something for nothing.

Hint: Use a public pay phone to place the ad, give the ad-taker at the paper that number, and then hang around a few moments since most newspapers require a call-back to check on the ad.

The same skit will work for firewood, too. This time the ad says: "Wife allergic to woodsmoke. Free firewood to be hauled away."

Newspapers

Late in 1985, fake copies of the *San Francisco Examiner* with a banner headline, "Peaceniks Seize Pentagon," were placed in about 100 newsracks in the city's financial and Civic Center districts.

A phony front page wrapped around old *Examiner* copies was similar to the real thing. The page carried teaser headlines for non-existent stories on the non-existent inside pages. Among them were "TV-Cancer Link Discovered" and "Missouri Loves Company — Nimitz Coming Too," a reference to the city's fight over stationing the battleship Missouri in San Francisco. There also was reference to the fortieth anniversary of the atom bombing of Nagasaki.

The pranksters, who have remained unidentified, also jammed the coin slots so readers could get a free paper.

Obscene Telephone Calls

Personally, I love 'em, but never seem to get any —
obscene phone calls, that is. Is it my personality or that
women never make any obscene calls? Yes, I know, a lot
of ladies do get them and don't like that and want to
know what to do. Here's the Largo Bum to the rescue.

"This works best with the guy who wants to meet
you somewhere. I refer to him as the Purpose Caller. It's
risky, but I advise you to encourage him a little, and
then tell him you'll meet him in two hours. Give him the
address of the nearest biker bar or police station — and
then have the place staked out by the inhabitants
therein."

Packages

Maybe your mark is a lonely sort of person because of the severe personality defect that caused him or her to become your mark. With that neat reasoning, Jay from Illinois has a kind suggestion on how your mark can meet many new friends. In humane fashion, Jay suggests, "Call fifty different people and tell each one of them that there is a special package waiting for him at the mark's house. Give the address. Try for odd-hour pickups, if you can. Or, if the mark is not without friends, schedule parcel pickup for a day he is having a party."

What's this? You say there's been a real death in the mark's family? You really hate this mark? If I may add a Hayduke refinement, *that* is the day to have the "packages" picked up — funeral day.

Paint

It's yet another landlord beef. This time, the owner told the tenant his rental place wouldn't be painted "this year because there's only enough money to paint one house, and it's going to be my own home." The tenant offered to do the painting if the landlord would buy the product. The landlord laughed and said: (1) wait until next year, (2) buy the paint yourself and do it yourself, (3) live with it, (4) move. The tenant, who calls herself Scorpion, had a fifth option.

"I remember my high-school chemistry teacher telling us about compounds which do nasty things to paint. I quickly found after a bit of label reading and experimenting that most shaving creams will bleach paint.

"Guess whose house got a bleach job a day or so after being painted? He blamed it on the paint and got into a ruckus with the store owner. It got to small claims court and the landlord lost. No proof. In the meantime I had moved."

Pear Trees

Although this is categorized as pear, it will work well with any fruit tree. It just happened that Raymond F. had first fruition with this gag on a pear tree. Years ago, he had this cranky old phart neighbor who terrorized the neighborhood kids if they picked pears from his tree. However, the kids learned that the old duffer did not really own the land the trees were on. He pretended to own the fruit trees, but, in reality, they belonged to the city.

The plot ripens . . .

Raymond explains, "We told our parents we wouldn't pick the pears anyway. For some reason, the parents didn't want to irritate this old turd, but I can't imagine why not.

"We didn't pick the pears. We ate them while they were on the tree — it was a dwarf tree. We simply ate all the fruit and left the stem part hanging on the tree."

Personal Products

Go through those mail-order catalogs and find personal products to gift-order for your mark. Always order COD, of course. Send your mark a gift card before the product arrives telling the mark that his or her friends suggested this personal gift or are getting it for "his or her own good." Make it one of those "your friends don't know how to tell you, but . . ." cards.

The COD "gift" will be something like nose hair clippers, vacuum blackhead/pimple remover, Accu-Jac masturbator, body hair remover, bust enhancers, cellulite cream, etc. Even if the parcel is COD, the curiosity of 95 percent of all marks will demand they pick up the package because of the card you sent. It works.

Pets

Fred Rogers said on TV that everyone needs a pet. If one pet is nice, think how wonderful 312 of them would be. You could easily make arrangements to have a steady supply of pets delivered to your mark each week. These can range from the exotic at various pet stores to the irregular mongrel models at animal shelters to ???? whatever.

Obviously, this requires a lot of research and lots of hype. You will have to comb the classifieds in several newspapers as well as the Yellow Pages in several directories. Not to worry about the well-being of the animals. The mark will never accept or keep any of them after the initial deliveries. After that, it is pure harassment value time.

Photofinishing

Way back in *Up Yours!*, Jimi the Z suggested loading bulk Kodak Kodalith film into 35mm cassettes and shipping them off to some photo finisher who has done you wrong. Several people have written in happily to tell me how well it works in screwing up the C-41 chemicals used by these derelict photo finishers.

Captain Video has been using empty Scotch 35mm film cassettes, also a C-41 process. He switches the film and sends the Kodalith in the Scotch container to any lab that has screwed him.

I can give it my own seal of approval. A lab not only ruined some film I had taken during a trip south of several borders, but told me it was my fault for not exposing my film properly and allowing customs people to x-ray, and thereby ruin the film. Nonsense. I have worked as a professional photographer and I do not allow my film supply to pass through X-ray. It is hand-inspected. The lab manager and I argued. He told me to buzz off.

Instead, I sent in four rolls of Kodalith in other cassettes, using the names of four other semi-marks. I had no intention of ever going back there and had

friends take in the film. I bet they have had a lot of annoyed customers recently.

Pinball Machines

Any of you video-arcade freaks ever see an old-fashioned pinball machine? Just kidding. Seriously, if you've ever been ripped off by the very "professional management" at one of these subhuman hangouts, thank Ray from Kansas City for his drill on getting even with them. Here's the idea.

Take a heavy rubber band and a piece of buckshot. Place the rubber band and buckshot over the payoff hole on the board. Pull the rubber band back and shoot the buckshot at the glass. You can place the rubber band right down flush on the glass and let it strike.

It will make a funnel-shaped nick in the glass with a small hole at the top. A bicycle spoke or a straight piece of wire may be inserted into the hole in the glass and on down to the copper contact in the payoff hole. Merely press on the wire and the score will begin to register. There is no hazard with electrical shock since the voltage at the contact point is only 3.6 volts, less than an ordinary flashlight. This can be worked even in busy locations using several people to stand around the machine while this is being performed.

Plants

A lot of fussy marks have fussy houseplants, the same as certain species of people have cats or small rat-like dogs. Tony from Illinois has a fun way of fertilizing some mirth into his life. He adds an Alka Seltzer tablet or so to each of the mark's houseplants, being careful to push each tablet under the soil. When the mark waters the plant, all sorts of hissing and bubbling will break the surface of the soil as the Alka Seltzer activates.

Tony adds, "I did this to a neighbor whose dog had totally dug up my bulb beds. She freaked out when the soil bubbled over in her plants that I had hit with the tablets. I was actually there and acting very concerned. Then I did it a couple of more times. She never caught on. She finally did tie up the dog, though. I still hit her plants a few more times just to piss her off. I didn't like her at all."

Plastic Money

At last, new games you can perform on your mark's credit cards. You owe the Lord God of Vengeance for these two ideas. He says that a large magnet placed near the mark's wallet or purse can zap, i.e., render useless, the magnetic strip on most credit cards. It erases the necessary codes. The LGV says this works best with cards for Automated Teller Machines (ATM).

Agreeing, Boston's Bart Phart says he once clamped a large block magnet just above the slot where people put their ATM cards. People thought it was just part of the equipment. He says it took thirty minutes for the bank to clear the complaints, figure out what was wrong, start to make amends, and order new cards — a one- to two-week wait.

Back to the LGV, he says that if you can get hold of your mark's plastic card, you can use a small screwdriver to alter numbers by pushing up or down on the raised plastic. He says you can turn 8 to 0, 7 to 1, etc. It makes shopping and banking less dull for the mark, of course.

Playing Cards

It was my army colleagues who taught me, finally, that I am a very poor card player. So, do you have problems winning, too? Have your "friends" cheated you? Captain Video has the answer — marked cards. He got nailed by some "buddies" who were dealing seconds to him. He later switched to this special deck I am mentioning here and cleaned out his cheating pal for 173 well-deserved dollars. If you're interested in obtaining a sealed set of these professionally marked cards, with instructions, see the *Sources* section under TPFC.

Poison Ivy

In the spring. when a young mark's fancy thoughts turn to plants and gardening, you can help the rash soul by substituting the usual flats of nice flower plants with some duplicates filled with seedlings of poison ivy.

I saw this work best on the public relations mouthpiece for a major coal corporation that was raping the land and destroying rural water supplies in western Pennsylvania. I was on a holiday visit with friends there in 1985 and again in 1986. The coal baron's paid liar's hobby was tending his own little flower garden far away from the embattled citizens who had no water because his company didn't give a damn where or how they deep-mined.

A friend of mine "somehow" added some poison ivy seedlings to the man's flats. The mark soon suffered one week of doctor-cared-for agony. I joined my friends and their neighbors in laughter. I urged them to send him a poison ivy bouquet as a "Get Worse" gift. As I was leaving that day, I'm not sure they actually did it. I hope so.

Politicians

I was sitting at a lemonade stand at an airport in Washington listening to some politician argue with a newspaper guy about why there should always be limits on press freedom. No lie, here's what the politico claimed: "Neither the substance of America's favorite sport, politics, or its favorite food, the hot dog, can stand close analysis. If the innards of either politics or the hot dog were fully revealed to the public, they'd vomit from reflex."

That's why Richard Nixon probably did say, "I never lied to you, I just economized with the facts."

From his bumper crop of brilliancy, Dick Smegma brings us another winner for dealing with political losers. This time he's getting you involved in a Hate a Candidate Campaign. Want to pay back a pol? You get hundreds of bumper stickers printed which favor this candidate or else steal his own stickers from a campaign headquarters. Make sure these are the superstick type that guarantee not to come loose. For that reason you may wish to have these custom-printed at a place using that type of sticker stock.

Next, you, or you and your crew, want to canvass

the town, placing as many of these stickers as possible on the trunk lids — never the bumpers — of every car you can locate. Or, you can place two on each car. The end result is beyond the obvious of losing votes for the candidate "whose" sticker you are disseminating. Some angry folks will threaten to sue. Also, the hoax will attract media attention.

Pornography

Again, leave it to Dick Smegma to come up with the most elaborate, long-range scheme I've ever encountered. Dick tells of a friend whose family is very open sexually as well as being nudists. The father used his two children (boy of ten, girl of twelve) to pose nude in softcore porno pictures. Being very sophisticated and experienced kids, they were hardly harmed by the experience. The father had a calendar page for the year 1996 printed for the photo session and made certain it was seen in all of the shots.

Dick says the father is saving the photos until 1996, when he is going to burn his mark with them. He will plant them on his mark, who is a very rotten hypocrite and a very powerful man in his region. Victims? All the police will find is the "current" photos, with calendar approval, and no realization that the young kids are actually now young adults.

Dick calls the guy a creative and patient genius. I agree. Dick also stresses that the family unit is very healthy, very happy, very mentally alert and in no way harmed by this. As I grow older, I find that most sexually repressed, and repressive, people tend to be certified mental cases. That's too bad . . . right, Edwin Meese?

That reminds me of one of Macho's school chiefs. As this headmaster at his NYC school was an obvious jerk-off, Macho sought and obtained secret access to the man's office. After sabotaging the liquor cabinet with additives, including ipecac, Macho next unpacked very explicit photos of naked people having a good time and taped them very securely to the *outside* of the window shades of the headmaster's bedroom, facing the neighbors' apartment side. Macho left. Needless to say . . .

During the investigation that followed the embarrassing incidents and situation involving the headmaster's room and booze supply, Macho and others were asked about their involvement. Macho reported to me, "I do declare, I can tell a lie."

Postal Stuff

Our consultant on cleaning up your postal budget by washing stamps has a new solution to cut costs. Buffy Bill says Mr. Clean, available in your supermarket, easily removes the cancellation inks used by the U.S. Postal Service. Bill also says that this is no lick in the wind, adding, "postal officials told Congress in 1985 that they had recovered a total of 13 million scrubbed stamps from big-time operators who were doing this stuff commercially. That has a value of $2.6 million."

Bill says that Mr. Clean works well to defeat the new inks the USPS uses to defeat the earlier washings. He also said it is highly unlikely their postal inspectors will ever go after the individual use of "sanitized" stamps.

Prey TV

I was a bit misty-eyed when I read that some wonderful electronics/computer expert named Edward Johnson had programmed his computer to make thousands of repeat calls to Jerry Falwell's 800 telephone number because this fund-grubbing electronic Bible-banger had taken large sums of money from the guy's mother. He ran up Falwell's bill to the pulsating amount of about $500,000.

It's wonderful, using that pious pride-in-the-pulpit's own 800 number to bill him for calls. Bells are ringing . . . hee, hee, dial 1-800-Revenge.

Little Tommie Titmouse really gets burned when he turns on his TV set to see something worthwhile and instead finds some rich, electronic frenzied preacher begging for more money to use to ruin our lives. Tommie has a neat stunt to bug these vidiots as well as a secondary mark. Here's how he does it.

"I go to a pay phone and call the toll-free number for each of these holier-than-thou types and pledge $50 to $100 in my secondary mark's name. I also give them his address. If they ask for the mark's phone number (as some do) to verify the call, I give them the pay phone. I stick around ten minutes or so, and about half the time they call back. I simply answer and identify myself by saying, 'Hello, Mr. Mark speaking,' and we talk awhile to verify I am who I say I am."

Tommie says that in the end, the mark might pay to avoid looking like a fool or to avoid confrontation with these right-wing frauds. Or if he doesn't pay, the vidiots send out their field reps to harass the mark. Either way, both deserved marks lose. Sometimes, Tommie says, they sue and countersue each other — more fun.

Pricks

The first time I'd ever heard of Aruba was when a bunch of the Soldiers of Misfortune had some sort of cockamamy operation planned to conquer this gorgeous island off the coast of Venezuela. I next heard about it from a very gorgeous lady known as the Aruba Palm Tree Lover who wishes she did own the place.

When Aruba Palm Tree Lover was very young, she dated this jerk who insulted her, abused her, used her, and cheated on her. Her response was chilling, in a manner of speaking. She warmed to her tale as she recalled the incident. "At that age and dating situation, hand-jobs were the most frequent type of casual sexual relationships for guys. Usually, a couple would use Vaseline, K-Y or baby oil.

"After I wised up to this jerk and found out what a real prick he was, I came to grip with things and came up with a new solution to the problem. I mixed in a good bit of odorless-type Ben Gay with the other lubricants. After a minute, he began to really get uncomfortable. Inside of two minutes, he was dashing for the bathroom and some soap and water. He never blamed me, but he never called back, either."

The very beautiful Aruba Palm Tree Lover also told me that she originally came from Newark, New Jersey, which would explain her nasty twist of mind. I have another friend who originally came from Newark, so I understood, right Pat?

Pubic Hair

As this series of books and I grow older, we're creating a family of friends. They progress and grow older, also. Remember our pal Tyra E. Pierce from rotten roommates fame in past books? Tyra has graduated now and is out in the unreal world, and still as creative as ever at getting back at the people who aren't nice to others. This time, Tyra suggests an ally common to most of us — pubic hair.

"One year I roomed with a neatness freak who was overly clean with everything but my stuff. He tossed my towels on the floor so he could hang up his. Sometimes he refused to flush my toilet, which he would fill with biological sculptures, so he wouldn't have to dirty his.

"That's when I found how much power common pubic hair has to gross out people, especially a neatness freak. Pubic hair is abundant, free, and easy to gather and use. I found that placing a lot of it on his toothbrush, soap, plates, pillow, etc., caused him to move out, soon. The secret, of course, is to use a different color and texture than that of the mark, or you can even use your own.

"Today, away from the college atmosphere, out

here working, I still find that our free friend, pubic hair, is quite useful in teaching manners to nasty people. My ultimate aim is for some secondary mark to stand up in a crowded mark-restaurant of my choice and scream, *"My God, there's a pubic hair in my soup!"*

Don't get lost, Tyra, you're our poet!

Meanwhile, beyond providing hirsute framing for Mr. and Ms. Johnson, pubic hair is a wonderful weapon for tasteless Haydukery that will, ahh, curl your mark's hair. Following are a few suggestions for the use of the short 'n curlies:

- If an old girlfriend or wife has some expensive facial creme, a handful of pubes mixed throughout the jar will toss that container, not to mention her cookies if you're truly blessed.

- A couple dark pubic hairs sticking out of the toothpaste tube when the lid is removed will cause your mark's teeth to chatter.

- Float 'em in someone's drink, soup, or cheese or any sort of icing, cookies, or other appropriate food.

- Stick pieces of pubic hair in your teeth and smile at someone you want to unnerve. This is fun to do if you want to make someone laugh, faint, or chunder at an inopportune time for them.

- Mail public hairs to your mark, either with or sans letter.

Quotes

"What's the meanest thing you've ever done to someone, George, then laughed about it?"

—David Fowler
WPLP Radio
Tampa Bay, Florida

"Age and treachery will always overcome youth and skill."

—Ronald Reagan
Mt. Sphincter, West Virginia

"Do you know how to really get even, George? Live long enough to become a problem to your own kids."

—A mother
Radio talk show
Chicago, Illinois

"Cut off the head of the leading concubine and the rest will behave."

—Sun Tzu
Whenever

"*Suo sibi gladio hunc jugulo* (I will cut this man's throat with his own sword.)"

—Terence
The Brothers
V, viii, 35

"The trouble with supping with the devil is that you must use a spoon twice as long as you need. In the end, it grows so long you cannot see the pot from which the food comes."

—Pope Something or other
The Vatican

Religion

Ilka Chase may not have known William Denton, but she called his shot when she said that "it is usually when men are at their most religious that they behave with the least sense and the greatest cruelty." While one church in particular has given Mr. Denton and his family a lot of grief, some of his get-back ideas will work with any religion. And, as I don't want to irritate His Popeness with William Denton's complaints, I will simply make this non-denominational.

The pay-back starts with rumors of a bootleg abortion clinic in the church neighborhood. This works best where the usual anti-abortion froth is at the mouther's nest. You compound the rumors by having some female friends with *big* tummy padding show up, spend an hour or two inside, then leave minus the padding. Refuse to let nosy neighbors near the house. Admit only your co-conspirators.

Finally, according to William Denton, you will start to attract pickets, police, and agitators. At this point, have the female friends come out with water balloons and attack the pious piglets who're picketing the "clinic."

Here's a somewhat less combative idea. Go to one of the church-related meetings and when the wimps and wimpesses start to glorify motherhood, you might ask why nuns can't be mothers and why some members of the clergy are not allowed to be biological fathers.

Restaurants

I actually saw this next trick performed by my friend, Ortega Beale. You need to have two slices of bread or toast handy. Spread some gooey jam on one slice very lightly and set it close by. Then lift the other slice to your nose as if it were a hanky. Blow your nose onto that slice, loudly and wetly. Make a demonstration of it. Spread the nasal contents around on the slice. Quickly switch slices and eat the one with the jam on it.

It happened one night that Lisa had simply had it with the teeny bopper waitri, plural of waitress, and their pimply paramours who stacked more hungry traffic behind the drive-up windows of the local Greaseburger franchise store than O'Hare does in a whole day of flight delay. Pushing chuckles of a runamuck chainsaw from her thoughts, Lisa brought her petite nail clippers from her purse and eyed the order-circuit speaker wire next to the large, illustrated display board next to her.

Snip.

"If you think the kiddy-cretins and their kissy-face held up business traffic, you should have seen my silencing of the whole system," Lisa said proudly, gently trimming her lovely, long red nails with the very same criminal clippers of a few hours earlier.

Rocketry

George Orr got really upset with some sorority pledges, calling them Nancy's kids after the wife of our Leader, because they were singing and chanting their nonsense at an hour when he was trying to sleep. George says that calls to the University of New Hampshire establishment to complain brought scorn from the fascists there. So, George acted on his own.

"The next night, when those chantresses started, I broke out my Wrist Rocket. Then I taped two pennies to each large M-60 I had, both for stability in distance and for shatter effect, and loaded one in my launcher. I had a friend light the explosive, then let fly with the missile toward the noisy women's large windows."

Crash! KARRBOOOOM!!!! This was followed by silence and George went back to sleep.

Satellite Television

One of the mean stories of 1986 was the scrambling issue involving satellite dish owners and the money-greedy biggies at HBO (Time/Life), CBS, Showtime, The Movie Channel, and others who scrambled their signals to shut out millions of rural dish owners who cannot get cable TV or any signal otherwise. It was a sad situation in which the rich telecasting monopolies got moreso and the poor, rural folks got shut out. The government? Forget it — they're part of the rich.

All of this brings me to a really hilarious incident that happened in April of 1986, when someone calling himself Capt. Midnight actually cut in on and blocked out the HBO signal one Sunday night to make his own declaration of war on the avaricious scramblers. He vowed to strike again.

Now, here's what I'd like to know: Are there any satellite hackers out there reading this book who could come up with ideas for Hayduking these greedy telecasting biggies who scramble for *big* profits? I'd very much like to hear from you, and anything useful will go in my next volume of fun and infame. Speaking of those greedy jerks reminds me of the next topic.

Septic Tanks

Von Henry had (note use of past tense) a lot of hassle with a person who dumped refuse on his property. The usual complaint and cheek-turning failed to stop the dumping, so Von turned a new leaf, rather than his cheek. "I located the mark's own home and noted he had a septic tank system with a clean-out opening between the house and the tank itself," Von recalls. "I found that a couple of spray cans of that foam insulation worked really well once it hardened and plugged the pipe."

That immediately reminded me of something the very wonderful Linda Ellerbee, who outgrew NBC-mentality, once said about septic tanks that very much relates to the principles that sometimes guide my actions in revenge. Linda said, "In a septic tank the really big chunks always rise to the top, while it's usually the smaller pieces that clog the system." I wonder if that was her metaphor for the networks, too?

Sex Toys

Because so much of sexual matters involve the ego, libido, and a person's other mental parts, sex toys can be used to your advantage when messing up someone's mind. I learned a lot about this while sharing a radio talk show with the sex therapist Donna Muller, who is a gorgeous, Double C version of Dr. Ruth. This lady's Made in the U.S.A., though. Anyway, she says if you have an ex-sweetie, ex-luster, or someone to whom you owe a mind-screwing (the editor made me change the original word), sexual paraphernalia — fun toys for inventive girls and boys — can be a good weapon.

"You can mail-order him a dildo along with a Get Well or Sorry about Your Illness card. You can sign your or someone else's name. Or, sign no name. Sign it 'Frustrated with Limp Wimp,' something like that.

"Or, send him an Accu Jac, a penis enlarger, or Stay Hard pills. You can do this to her, too, Peruse some of the personal ads in the more explicit sex magazines and you'll find just the ticket," Muller advised.

One of her favorites involved one of her slutty friends who was making her husband's life miserable by openly shacking around. Muller dummied up a very realistic-looking letterhead from a local motel and created a Frequent Customer Club for her mark/friend to belong to. She sent it to her lady mark at the office where she was an executive, knowing full well the secretaries would have the gossip around in no time.

Included with the letter was a very explicit catalog of very kinky sex toys from the famed Postal Palace of Porno, owned by Hulk McCutcheon, one-time pro-wrestling villain.

Shell Casings

Our Jimmy Carter was ripped off by a scumbag merchant in his city and did all the nice, polite things to get the deal righted. The creep just laughed at Jimmy. Jimmy went to a nearby rifle range and borrowed a dozen or so empty rifle cartridge casings of various calibers. He wired a little message tag to each one and began having them mailed to the salesman/mark from different parts of the country. Some of the tags read:

- My loaded brother has your name on it.
- Next time, you get my bullet . . . in your ass.
- Just the right size for a crooked cheater.
- I'm way above your caliber . . . but you'll still be dead.

You probably get the idea. Jimmy cautions you that the authorities would probably take almost as dim a view of this as will the mark. He suggests you be very careful with prints, handwriting/typing, etc.

Shoplifting

If you know one or more of the stores that your mark frequently patronizes, you can add his/her name to that store's list of known shoplifters. It's easy if you work there or know someone who does. It's also a rotten trick that will cause much unhappiness to fly back and forth between accused and accuser when the confrontation finally happens.

In another variation of this, Ronnie Lenguin says to create some local police department letterhead using a photocopying machine and some purloined originals. Create a warning letter from the local police naming your mark as a major shoplifter. Send this letter to various local shops or leave them lying around your mark's office.

Smokers

Smokers are as out of place in my life as George Bush's clip-on bowties would be at a Paris fashion show. So, here is an easy get-back. Prick a number of very small holes in the fag (the cigarette, you klutz) near the filter area. When the smoker/mark inhales, he will pull in mostly air from those undetected holes and wonder what's wrong with his smoke. If this doesn't work, douse the mark with a gallon of gasoline from a very safe distance once he or she lights up. Whoa, just kidding . . .

Barney Vinceletti has a charming elevator story about another non-smoker who tired of ingesting the stale poisons that these lung killers leave around. Barney says the friend targeted this sand-filled ashtray in the elevator in his apartment building by replacing the sand with a mixture of potassium nitrate and sugar.

As Barney added, "You could experiment with the mixture, but my pal left just enough there to scare the hell out of the smokers on board next time. If you want to be more conservative, you can leave used condoms in those ashtrays . . . fill 'em with milk or whatever. Personally, I prefer the nastier approach."

Sneezing and Coughing

Pat Buchanan is a fourth-grade-level class clown who never got out of high school, even after he graduated. You know the type . . . if the world were a bottle of Dom Perignon he would be an aluminum screw top. Well, I was almost embarrassed to pass this along, until a friend, whom I respect as a real trickster, suggested the same thing. That lets me off the hook.

Sometimes, an obscene sneeze is in order, but don't ask *me* when or where. When you feel a real sneeze coming on, go in your usual loud voice, *"Fah . . . fah . . . fah . . . fah . . . fah . . . faw . . . KEW!"* Or, when you have to cough, you simply cough the word *Kotex* very loudly.

Please don't ask me to go over that again.

Sources

Listing these sources is not my endorsement of them, or the people, products, and services, unless noted as such. I suggest you shop around and ask for information if there are several sources listed as there are varied prices, often for the same items and services. Some will sell and ship all products, others will not. It's best to ask questions first.

Abbeon Cal, Inc., 123-285Y Gray Avenue, Santa Barbara, CA 93101

> Mark permanently with real paint pens, and here's where you can get them. They wholesale the real thing in all colors.

Alcan Wholesalers, Inc., P.O. Box 2187, Bellingham, WA 98227

> Holy gung ho! These guys have a catalog crammed full of police, military, and security goodies; equipment; ID; chemicals; and supplies. They're real.

Badge-A-Minit, Ltd., 348 N. 30th Road, La Salle, IL 61301

> Buttons and badges make great personal graffiti, but some outfits censor what you want to be

printed. Solution? Buy your own machine and make your own. The price of a badge/button machine and starter kit is less than $25.

Baron Samedi, Box 2084, Glenview, IL 60025
This evil chap guarantees "voodoo revenge" on your enemies. Anywhere, anyone, and fast. Guaranteed for only $25.

Baytronics, Box 591, Sandusky, OH 44870
Vets especially will appreciate the huge stocks of GI surplus commo equipment here, some of it very modern. They have all sorts of communication gear.

BBN, Box 4675, Akron, OH 44310
Advertised as an effective chemical castration solution, this product is advertised as being available from these folks for $5 per dose.

Blackhawk, Rt. 1, Box 221, Blue River, WI 53518
A chemical supply house that sells hard-to-find goodies by mail. When I last looked, chloroform was featured at two ounces for $5.

Break Wind Enterprises, Box 77, Mount Ida, AR 71957
These people sell all sorts of fart-related gadgets, signs, and bumper stickers. They're my kind of tasteful folks.

Bullshippers, 1232 Kenwood Dr., Bluffton, IN 46714
Humiliated and angry? Hate someone? Send them a Crap-O-Gram. Enjoy the sweet smell of success against your mark when these folks deliver a nasty gift card message and a gift-wrapped box of fake (I wonder) cowshit.

Bumper, Box 22791, Tampa, FL 33622
Bumper stickers are the literature of American philosophy as we head into the final decade of this century. Depressing. Yet, many companies will print whatever you wish, however you wish without worrying about what you say. That is remarkably open-minded in these days of religious persecution and political censorship.

Cardinal Publishing, 2071 Emerson, Jacksonville, FL 32207

If you need blank certificates, here they are — birth, baptismal, marriage/divorce, wills, awards, diplomas, etc.

CRB, Box 56, Commack, NY 11725

Hear the feds before they hear or find you! CRB sells books and equipment that reveal all the "secret" frequencies of the FBI, CIA, ATF, FCC, customs, and the military. This is like a big supermarket for buggers, antibuggers, and others who want to know who is listening to what and why.

Dwan Starks, 515 Byrne St., Petersburg, VA 23803

Learn the secrets of locksmithery (aka lock picking), with books, instructions, tools, accessories and equipment. A starter kit is available for $5.

EarthFirst!, P.O. Box 5871, Tucson, AZ 85703

This is David Foreman's magnificent journal of monkey-wrenching, aka ecological sabotage. It is a grand magazine for activists who want to stop the rape and pillage of our land.

Eden Press, P.O. Box 8410, Fountain Valley, CA 92728

Their motto is that living privately is best and their books support that motto. This seller of books has a catalog selection ranging from insuring your privacy to invading someone else's. How to set up a business, live in the underground economy, or mess up someone else — it's all there, including my books.

Ephemera, Inc., 275 Capp St., San Francisco, CA 94110

Perverted and disgusting buttons are the forte here, and they also do custom work. Bad taste is their hallmark.

Freedom Press, Box 2451, Farmington Hills, MI 48024

This place is like having access to a major library on chemical, biological and explosive warfare. They sell how-to books, plans and formulas, and they are good folks.

Funny Side Up, 425 Stump Rd., North Wales, PA 19454
This is an adult version of the old Johnson Smith catalog. You need a copy of this class clown's bible.

Gims, Box 45212-452, Baton Rouge, LA 70816
Fill up your funster's first-aid kit from this legitimate wholesale medical supply house, which sells medical treatment equipment and supplies. A catalog costs $5 (refundable with order).

Inkadinkado, Inc., 105 South St., Boston, MA 02111
Rubber stamps + your imagination = grand fun. These people furnish hundreds of splendid, creative, and custom rubber stamps and accessories. The rest is up to your wonderful mind.

ITC, Inc., Box M508, Hoboken, NJ 07030
Bugged by someone's sexual stunts or you want to use sexual rumor to fornicate up a mark? These guys have two official-looking stickers for sale. One says V.D. Clinic — Urgent Report, the other says Dirty Book Club Application Form. Give 'em a dose of their own.

Kansas City Vaccine Co., P.O. Box 5713, Kansas City, MO 64102
These folks sell all pet products and drugs — real drugs. One item that may interest you is rabies vaccine.

A.B. Kaufman, Box 140, Livingston, NJ 07039
Are you also pissed off at the incredible rip-off known in the TV industry as signal scrambling? If you want to know the entire issue truth as well as own a catalog full of solutions contact Kaufman.

Keller Sales, P.O. Box 215, Logan, Utah 84321
Fireworks and fireworks components are available from these fine folks at reasonable prices.

Kephart Publications, 495 Pleasant Valley, Murphy, NC 28906
These are the folks who sell simple plans for some

very exotic weapons you can make in your own home workshop for very little money. The stuff looks pretty neat, too.

Lindsay Publications, Inc., P.O. Box 12, Bradley, IL 60915

This is a very interesting publishing house, offering a lot of old-fashioned how-to books for the person who wants to be independent and self-reliant. There are all sorts of technical goodies available here and the catalog is free.

Loompanics, Unlimited, P.O. Box 1197, Port Townsend, WA 98368

This is a major one-stop shopping center for all of the great books on topics even remotely related to our business here. In his catalog, Mike Hoy has created a bibliography of the most exotic, arcane, bizarre, and neat books available. If it's published, Loompanics has it. These folks are Four Star Hayduke Approved.

Male Order Photolabs, 18718 Ventura Blvd., Tarzana, CA 91356

This lab will process your sexually explicit photographs and get them back to you safely. The cost is $8.95 per twenty-four exposures, plus a buck for postage. They accept MC and VISA. They're OK.

Mesa Books, Drawer 1798-AX. Denver, CO 80201

Choose from a list of more than five dozen booklets loosely related to survival and nastiness to your enemies. The incredible price is just $1 per booklet — neat titles, too. Their motto is "Ban Defeat." I can get into that.

Norstarr, P.O. Box 5585, Pocatello, ID 83202

Make your own explosives and fireworks. They supply everything, including instructions, formulae, and all ingredients for explosives, smoke dyes, etc. Catalog is $1.

Nelson-Hall Publishing, 111 Canal St., Chicago, IL 60606

In addition to their run-of-the-press trade books, these folks published a wonderfully useful book by Roland Baker, *The Liar's Manual*. Check your bookstore and somehow get a copy. It is a fantastic manual for building a trickster's attitude. It's not a cookbook of recipes; rather, it's a gourmet mind-builder.

Nova Detection Systems, 11684 Ventura Blvd., Studio City, CA 91604

Need a telephone line transmitter? They sell a kit that is a very dangerous threat to your mark's privacy.

On The Nose, P.O. Box 1588, San Pedro, CA 90731

They sell various odors, both natural and chemical. I hardly need to tell you what that means. I am sure you'll find dozens of uses for their smelly products.

Overthrow, P.O. Box 392, Canal Street Station, New York, NY 10013

The official newspaper of the Youth International Party (Yippies), this great publication contains more truth than many straight media. I've been a satisfied reader for years. It's worth the price of a subscription, well worth it.

Paladin Press, P.O. Box 1307, Boulder, CO 80306

Paladin's the top publisher for the kind of books you need to plan the perfect revenge. A publisher of the Hayduke library of revenge master-pieces, Paladin shows you how to protect your right to live, and how to make or get the tools to do it right.

PBS Livestock Drugs, 2800 Leemont Avenue, Canton, OH 44711

If your mark may be considered livestock, you will find PBS a sweet source of biologicals and other veterinary drugs and products. They have a $1 catalog with some disturbing implements and medicines for sale.

Peter Productions, Box 218, Stratford, CT 06497

Farts are fun and make a great Haydukery tool. An authentic tape of magnificent flatulence is very valuable. I've heard thousands of the real thing and this tape is authentic and classic. It's only $6 — cheap!!

Phoenix Systems, Inc., P.O. Box 3339, Evergreen, CO 80439

This is the real thing for all of you who follow true liberty and honesty, not that Sylvester "I ran off to Sweden" Rambo bull. This outfit has a whole lot of good military goodies, including parts, kits, manuals, and other stuff that nobody else seems to have the balls to sell. It's like a Contra K-Mart.

P & K Enterprises, Box 6155, Minneapolis, MN 55406

Their motto is "We print any message." And they do it on bumper stickers for a very reasonable price. Here's where you get those rotten personal bumper stickers printed for your mark's car.

P.W., 237 W. Houghton Lake Drive, Prudenville, MI 48651

Any message printed and no minimums for this bumper-sticker business. They sell 'em for two bucks each.

Seton Name Plate Corp., P.O. Drawer DF-1331, New Haven, CT 06505

This fine industrial firm has a huge catalog of plastic and metal signs — identification products. These are stick-ons, bolt-ons, etc., and they look real because they *are* real.

Shotgun News, P.O. Box 669, Hastings, NB 68901

It's 100 percent advertising and the world's greatest single source of guns, knives, etc. This is the gun nut's bible.

SME, P.O. Box 251, Warren, OH 44482

Ohio must be the explosives center of the U.S. Here is yet another buckeye boomer offering all sorts of blow-em-up goodies, smoke grenades, etc. Send SASE for custom specs and consulting, too.

Ron Smith Productions, 9000 Sunset Blvd., Hollywood, CA 90069

This is the man with more than 500 doubles and talented impressionists for the celebrities of yesterday and today.

Sooner Supply, Box.454, Lawton, OK 73502

A handyfolk's supply of chemicals, casings, and other supplies to make fireworks. Their catalog costs you a buck.

Sunsponges, Box 20782, San Diego, CA 92120

Hmmm, this comes close to ripping off old George, but I'm the sweet kind of guy who laughs at it anyway. The people are selling stick-on artwork of screws. They replace those damned cutesy heart stickers. Or, make up your own use (see *Bumper stickers* for one use).

Top Drawer Rubber Stamp Co., Box 38, Hancock, VT 05748

We've all seen the cute, the historic, and the artsy rubber stamps for sale. Now, a company is offering the sick, black, and bizarre, e.g., hanging corpses, spiders, mutilations, and one saying, "Pay or Die." I like these — they're awful.

TPFC, Inc., 3734 Burlington Avenue North, Suite #1, St. Petersburg, FL 33713

These folks sell you a deck of professionally marked rewrapped cards, as original Bicycle brand playing cards for $8. Each deck comes with instructions and is guaranteed to get you $$$ even with your cheating enemies.

Trident, 2875 South Orleans, Milwaukee, WI 53227

This is a mail-order chemical house with lots of fun stuff at fair prices. Send your wants and SASE.

Uniquity, 215 4th St., Galt, CA 95632

Need to make a statement to a verbal bully? Work with a brain-dead someone whose mouth runs all the time? Does the verbal excrement of politicians bore you? Try *Bullshit Repellent,* the product that comes in a spray can to disperse even the most stubborn verbal effluvia. It's only $6.50 a can.

Walter Drake, The Drake Building, Colorado Springs, CO 80940

This is one of those little catalogs your mother gets, full of cutesy gifts and novelty items for the house. It also is a Hayduker's delight — lots of custom-printed and specialty items useful for dealing with marks. It's one of my favorites.

WASP, P.O. Box 5091-AB, Steamboat Springs, CO 80477

Invest $5 in this catalog of discounted medical supplies and equipment. They sell all sorts of drugs, supplies, instruments, and medicines at cheap prices.

The Wild Geese, Postfach 1145, 6460 Gelnhausen, Federal Republic of Germany.

These folks do some publishing and claim to be on the cutting edge of mercenarydom, but that may be a shill. Whatever, they offer some wonderful printing services, including death warrants, search warrants, interesting ID cards, etc.

YS & Company, P.O. Box 6713, Salinas, CA 93912

Give yourself an alibi with one of the taped, sound-effect cuts on this company's cassettes. Great background sounds to play in the background of your telephone calls. I have this product — it's very useful.

If you have a product, service or whatever that you think would be useful for readers of my books, let me know. Tell me about it via letter and/or send a sample for the next book. Many of these listings are from readers who notified me in this way.

Spray Paint

If you think gun laws make no sense, you need to meet Artha Woods, a councilwoman from Cleveland, Ohio, who proposed local legislation which would require the registration of people who buy cans of spray paint. The lady said she was tired of seeing graffiti sprayed all over Cleveland and thought police could easily track down the authors of new graffiti by tracing their spray paint cans.

The *Spokesman-Review* of Spokane, Washington, reported that officials in Los Angeles and in Spokane were considering the same legislation. The Spokane newspaper commented in its editorial, "People don't cause graffiti, spray paint does."

In 1986, the Los Angeles city council proposed a ten-cent-per-can tax on spray paint to pay for graffiti removal. Would it be cheaper to remove inept and incompetent politicians? I guess so, the 10¢ tax measure failed.

It's obvious that when paint is outlawed, only outlaws will have paint. Or, when lawful painters have to register their cans, only criminals will paint graffiti. Or, will painters spray outlaws or become outlaws?

Whadaya think, Artha? I'm kind of confused, which puts me in your league, I suspect. Have you registered your can, Artha?

Stencils

This idea is especially useful if you want to get back at someone who's spreading nasty lies and rumors about you or a friend. It's brought to you through the courtesy of Dick Smegma. You obtain a stencil with a message something like this:

JOHN JERKOFF
555-1212
1234 Anystreet
Histown
MOLESTS KIDDIES

Or, you can accuse him or her of having sexual relations with dead animals, with desecrating churches, bombing synagogues, torching an orphanage, or some other vile act. Hold your stencil up against any smooth-surfaced wall and let go with a blast of spray paint, peeling away the stencil. Instant smear campaign.

Strobes 'n Stereos

Does your mark enjoy the old disco bit with strobes or are there strobes in ye old markhome? If so, Dr. Deviant says you can use this strobe to drive your mark into near seizure if you can guarantee captive response.

The Doctor advises, "Any strobe light set between ten and twenty-five flashes per second will induce a temporary seizure in most people. The affected nerves just can't keep up and they shut down, causing a bad-appearing seizure situation."

Again, I checked this with my medical consultant, Dr. Chris Doyle, director of the Dr. George Holiday Sanitarium, who confirmed the ten to twenty-five flashes dose. While on the subject, Dr. Doyle had a related suggestion.

"If your disco-mark also has a mind-boggling stereo system — most do — and it annoys the hell out of you, use it to pay back. If the mark is a heavy sleeper, put the headset over his ears. Otherwise, move the big speakers right up to the bed and surround the mark if you can.

"Then, hook that monster system up to the alarm and set it for some horrible hour that will cause maximum unhappiness to the mark, not to mention ear damage. Crank up the volume, set the alarm to ON, and leave with a smile on your face."

Stupid "Success" Story

The most stupid success story since the last book came to me from a reader in Harrisburg, Pennsylvania, who sent me a clip about some dunderhead who dressed up in an ape costume and was going around scaring people in a rural area near that state's capital city.

Local police were quoted as saying, "Citizens who've seen it say it isn't human . . . a six-and-a-half-foot hairy creature with long arms and big fangs. Personally, we think this creature came out of costume shop, rather than a deep swamp."

Seems they were right. Checks with Harrisburg costume-shop records turned up leads that led to an arrest on various charges. Why was this a stupid stunt? First, the buyer shopped locally and used his own name and address on sales records. But, the most absolutely stupid thing the guy did was to pull off this stunt in a rural area of Pennsylvania, a state which has more licensed hunters and gun owners than any other in the nation.

Boom! Boom! Potential end of prank.

The guy was lucky to end up being tried by twelve rather than carried by six.

Stupid "Success" Story, Pt. II

A lot of times radio show hosts ask me about such words as illegal, guilty, law, and other such terms as once faced one of history's master dirty tricksters, Richard "I am not a crook" Nixon. I always tell them that you can't be guilty unless you're caught and proved to have done something illegal, as so many distinguished citizens prove in and out of our courts every day. So, I am not sure we can call this a success story; I guess that is up to the principals involved. Perhaps, it was best identified by San Francisco's RB who first sent me the newspaper clip. RB called it "Haydukery at work."

In the small town of San Carlos, about 30 miles south of San Francisco, an ex-police officer and his son were charged with criminal libel early in 1986 for forging the police chief's signature to a racist political campaign letter in a local election the year before.

According to local officials, the letter was a lie and the defendants had a history of holding grudges against people with whom they'd had a dispute. In addition to the letter, the son was also charged with dumping "an odorous mixture of blue cheese and ammonia" in the city hall-police department ventilation system, and with spray-painting nasty anti-police graffiti on downtown buildings.

According to local officials, the two men may have been getting scenarios for their vendettas from a how-to book found in their home by investigators. That book is titled *Get Even,* according to the newspaper account.

After studying that newspaper clipping, I found all kinds of stupid decisions made by these two losers. But, maybe it was all just in fun.

Subversives

Ahahah, now there is a term from the McCarthy era! But, as I write this, we are in a neo-McCarthy era, so, what the hell? Here is a refinement for the crank letter idea of *Make 'Em Pay!* You "have" your mark write letters of praise, wish-to-join and to pledge money to all of the Communist, crank church, neo-Nazi, etc, groups. These efforts will also draw the attention of various snoopy governmental agencies.

Success Stories

I cannot go into detail because of both the newness and the nearness, but I can tell you that our old veteran contributor, The Skull, has used Haydukery to the utmost to create a demolishing hell for a woman who totally messed him up personally and financially on a rental deal. You will have to take my word for the fact that he did her in with a classic combination of techniques. Perhaps in some issue down the publication line I can provide details. Otherwise, The Skull holds a High Five for 100 percent success in a *big* win.

Dr. Barry Lebetkin is director of the Institute for Behavior Therapy in New York City, an upright place, and not some CIA shrink front for illegal assassination stuff like it sounds. Dr. Lubetkin says, "There are certain situations where people feel justifiably vengeful and no amount of talking to them about forgetting about getting even works. It's probably healthy to some degree."

Later, the good Doctor mentioned a patient who told him that he once put liquid cement in the door locks of twenty new cars at a dealership where he'd been way overcharged for repairs, then given no satisfaction with his complaint. Dr. Lubetkin added, "The patient said he got the idea from some funny book on getting even with enemies."

Is that flattery, or what, folks?

It's nice to know people do have a sense of humor in South Carolina. In February 1986, a South Carolina couple offered a $5,000 reward for the person who swiped a personal photo showing the lady topless and then printed it in a brochure inviting hundreds of people to a "sex orgy" at the couple's home.

The two-page brochure, which was professionally done, also showed four other photos, out of focus, but clearly of explicit sex acts. They were mailed to 200 people, including friends of the couple, their pastor, and business acquaintances. The copy in the brochure invited recipients to come have a swinging sexual time with the couple and their guests.

And, speaking of publications, here's grand news. Barney Vinceletti got his first novel published and "it offends almost every icon of society" as Barney puts it. I read it, he's right. It's called *The Bird of Paradise*.

Super Glues

By now, everyone in the nation claims to actually know some guy who had his Mr. Happy super-glued to his leg, a phenomenon which reminds me of the veracity of the Westmoreland Bodycount System in Vietnam. Back in the world of reality, though, the fabulous La Croix Bothers muse on a new method of getting folks to stick around after a robbery, Haydukery, or whatever. Their idea is simple: "You put a dab of a super glue on each fingertip of each mark, then make certain each mark presses those fingertips hard against a flat wall for thirty seconds. Then it's bye-bye time for you."

In this case, parting really will be such sweet sorrow for the mark(s), which is why you have to hand it to the Brothers LaCroix for this stunt.

Supermarkets

Dick Smegma liked our food fight scam from *Make 'Em Pay!* but also has one of his own that works everytime. It's simple. When you need to extract revenge upon a market, grab an unused PA microphone or telephone in a quiet area of the store and use your own version of this generic script:

"Attention Food Circus Shoppers. To make room for incoming stock and for the next ten minutes only, we have a *Super Special* on fresh, whole milk — only 25¢ per gallon. That's right. Only 25¢ per gallon — buy all you want for the next ten minutes."

Instant chaos everytime, Dick adds.

Our supersnooper, Captain Video, has been prowling the revenge section of his least favorite market again and has come up with another Black Light Special.

"Did you know that the 6½-ounce cans of cat food and of chunk light tuna are exactly the same container?" the good Captain asks rhetorically. "A bit of water applied to the glue sections of the label easily remove same without tearing. From there it is just an instant to switch the labels, re-attach, and resupply the supermarket shelves. Nobody is the wiser until Mark II opens whichever can."

Sweeties

Upon meeting Consuela, his brother's four-legged consort from Colon, Panama, Dr. David McGeary shuddered and said, "Lips that touch swine shall never touch mine." It's a nice sentiment, but old-fashioned. Now, let's see how others handled this old problem.

Being a good chap, Andrea knows some ladies. He told me a story about a friend of his who found his sweetie had hot pants for another guy — any guy. He decided to help. He placed a Tabasco-type sauce mixture in her liquid vaginal soap. A mysterious burning rash curtained her sexual adventures for a while. Funny thing, it would reoccur. Maybe, it was the guys she was shacked up with?

This next mark is one of the major hypocrites of our century. A staff member of the Meese Commission on Pornography, this doofuss was *also* a secret chaser of young skirts and knickers, an AC/DC slime. Mr. Justice saw a way to get even with this pious pillar of his fundamental church and head of his very proper household. Mr. Justice had a trusted female associate call this dork's unlisted home telephone number on a day they knew he was away and that Mrs. Wonderful was home.

The female friend identified herself as a doctor from a local, exclusive health clinic and asked to speak to the mark. Informed he was not at home, the "doctor" hemmed and hmmmed a bit, then came right out with it.

"You are Mrs. Mark? Well, I am sorry to be the one to tell you this, but as it concerns you, too, I guess you need to know." She went on to explain that the mark's AIDS and genital herpes tests were "generally negative," but that she (our "doctor") still wanted to talk to him about identifying the woman with whom he was involved because they had reason to believe she was a carrier.

Now that probably gave the old fun couple a few grists for conversation upon his arrival to the old hearthside, eh?

Not nearly as mean, but a sure barb at the other half's suspicion quotient, is the mistaken identity gambit. Tommy Tolar from Little Rock suggested it and here's how it unrolls. When your mark introduces Sweetie to you, look very puzzled, then say, slowly, "Ahhh, this isn't the same lady/man you introduced me to last _____?" (*Pause, then smile, punch mark playfully in the arm, and say,*) You old hot pants, you. Wow, you sure know how to pick 'em." Then proceed with embarrassing, personal comments of a generally sexist nature.

Paulette Cooper has a nice touch for an errant spouse whom you wish to make your mark in a support case. It's easy. You simply make sure the mark's correct name, but wrong address, are recorded for the support notices. That way, the mark never really hears about the money due, the hearings, all the rest. The next item may be an arrest notice, and that always gets through personally.

Paulette has another thought which is devastating in its simplicity. Your mark has a wife, live-in, or very close girlfriend. You send flowers to her in the man's name. He'll always wonder.

All of this probably caused my newlywed friend from New Orleans to remark, "It used to be wine, women, and song. Now, it's beer, the old lady, and TV." His marriage ought to go swimmingly, which reminds me . . .

Swimming Pools

More refinements keep pouring into the Hayduke pool of pustule. Carl called from Champaign, Illinois, to suggest putting several pounds of a product known as Mr. Bubble into a mark's swimming pool. It will feed through the filter and foam everything. It's tough to defoam, too, Carl claims.

Or, would you like to fill up a mark's pool with urine, but just can't make enough of the product? Try the almost next best thing — urine color and stench. I'd like to thank Hacer Polvo for this idea. Combine three parts yellow food coloring with one part green and two parts fox urine lure. Ye mark will think that the Jolly Peeing Giant just whizzen full the pool. It looks and smells just like an unflushed commode, Hacer says.

According to Missouri's Mr. Heffer, a nasty scavenger fish known as the carp will live in even heavily chlorinated water. It will also crap up a pool really well. Mr. Heffer says to toss some carp into the mark's pool when the mark is away for a weekend. Include some roadkill and other food for the fish. "Guaranteed, the mark will have to drain and totally clean that pool; it will be that bad," says Heffer. That's good.

Mr. Justice is a neat guy to invite to a pool party, especially one being hosted by your rude neighbor who likes *loud* music, and *obnoxious* guests, and doesn't mind sharing them with you, never mind that you don't want to be shared with. Mr. Justice acts after the party has ended, and, using a sharp knife, makes a major slash in the pool's vinyl liner near the bottom of the deep end. He then inserts a large piece of broken branch taken from a nearby tree, hopefully as in overhanging nearby, and jams it into the rapidly draining slash. The mark thinks the rip happened accidentally. But, you'll know better.

Mr. Justice also has ways for you to help your nasty mark winterize his pool, saying, "When the mark covers up and buttons down the pool for the winter, but doesn't drain it, you can help out by slipping some insulation under the cover and into the water." For insulation, Mr. Justice recommends things like roadkill; a gallon of used motor oil; garden fertilizer; large piles of dog, horse or cow poop; etc. Our helpful hero adds, "The mark literally will be able to walk on that water when he uncovers the pool the next spring."

Tampons

Yes, lovers of the nasty, there is even a Mrs. Skull out there in wonderful Warmland, USA. She passes along a fine idea if your mark is a woman, as opposed to a lady, and you want to really gross her out and disgust her. Mrs. Skull says to see that a couple of used tampons — used in any way you wish — are mailed, delivered, given, or whatever to Ms. Mark or to someone else in her name.

Make no bones about it, I would not want to cross Mrs. Skull!

Telephones

Dr. Yaz has a great way of turning a simple, kiddy telephone stunt into a very creative revenge tactic. It's the old silent phone call bit. He calls the mark and says nothing while the mark says hello half a dozen times before hanging up. Dr. Yaz, of course, is recording all of this on a high-quality machine. A couple replications of this tactic soon brings on cursing and swearing from the mark. Several more calls drew even more explicit and scatalogical threats — all of this recorded, of course.

"With a bit of judicious editing and some pre-framed questions also recorded on the telephone, we put together a nice tape which made this mark sound like a real foul-mouthed psychopath. Naturally, we sent copies of the tapes to his parents, girlfriend, teachers, minister, and family doctor," Dr. Yaz says.

Unless you have a bizarre sense of humor — and I guess you must or you wouldn't have gotten this far in this book — harassing phone calls aren't much fun for most people to receive. Personally, I love 'em because it's another chance to abuse some sicko and turn his vindication in reverse. Or, you can do what John Nothankyou from Phoenix did and turn a neat reversal of the calls to his own advantage by playing a mark. Don't be confused, read what John did.

"Most phone companies are very community-mindedly uptight about their customers being abused by harassing calls and are quick to help you get relief," John explains. "I use this willingness to punish my mark. Here's how.

"I call the phone company and pretend to be my mark. Obviously, I have to know a good bit about the mark and his/her phone number. I tell the company I have been getting nasty, threatening, sexual calls, etc. I tell them I don't want the police and I don't want a hassle; I just want a new, unlisted number.

"Every single time I have done this to a mark, it has worked! The company is pleased to satisfy me so easily. They immediately switch the mark's number and usually tell me what it is on the spot. Bingo."

Now the mark's friends and associates cannot call him. The mark will not know his or her own number . . . and you will. Think about it.

Chinese Gordon managed to knock out a corporate telephone switchboard once with just a few moments of access to the front of the board. His trick was to insert fine sprays of heavy mercury into the works by means of a small pressure device nozzle he managed to get between the console boards and frame, much like you'd caulk between seams of a building. He thus knocked out an entire telephone communication network. The mercury shorted the wiring, which superheated, boiled, and exploded the guts of the system.

Dick Smegma says that if you hang around any large airport with a pocket telescope, which is inexpensive and fits easily into your shirt pocket, you can carefully observe, with practice, people placing long-distance calls at pay phones, "punching in" their telephone credit card numbers on the phone buttons.

You should always pick someone who deserves this sort of thing being done to him, of course. Or, you can simply follow your mark and do this to him or her as a primary pay-back, obtaining the telephone credit card number, and making dozens of business calls from another public phone, using a mark's name and address during the conversation. For example, you could order merchandise to be shipped C.O.D.

Eventually, the mark whose telephone credit card number you "borrowed," will demand that the phone company investigate, and they will. They'll call the companies listed on the credit cardholder's bill, and their investigation will point to your mark's name and address.

Should someone at an airport ask what you're doing with a telescope, explain that you are with a private detective agency, and you are trailing some guy who is cheating on his wife or, vice versa.

In another version of the same thing, where you don't need the telescope and you're not known to your mark, you can pretend to make your own call from the neighboring telephone and let your eyes do the wandering and recording while the mark does his button pushing.

Toilets

Although most of us never went to the University of Arizona, I bet we all know someone like Tom. Stay on his good side. Tom says when you owe someone a toilet-tinged pay-back, open up the top of his water tank and dump a half box of laundry detergent in there. When the mark flushes the toilet, he gets a foam flood of washday miracle foaming up and up and up — all over the bowl and the floor. And, it just keeps on foaming and flowing.

Meanwhile, Jed Wisebooger, a used toilet sludge collector, once had this next stunt pulled on him, according to Bullet Bill. Tricksters who were furious with Jed for his cheating them on several business deals got to work in the basement beneath his living area. They uncoupled "his" toilet drain below the trap and rerouted the pipe out and down into the backseat window of Jed's company car.

Bullet Bill reports, "Jed spent that weekend at home with his derelict family, all of them eating, drinking, pooping, and peeing.

"When he went down to get into that car to go to work Monday, he found a four-wheeled, mobile septic tank in his driveway, despite the modest leakage at the door joints."

Toothpaste

Have a friend who's not very clean or nice about borrowing toilet articles? Or, want to pay back a mark who is super-clean about personal toilet articles? Lil' Tommy Toothpaste has a great revenge trick for you.

"Take your mark's partially empty toothpaste tube and carefully push small raisins up into the tube, mixed in with the paste. Do this about three or four times. The mark squeezes out toothpaste that night and these horrible, mangled gooshy things come splooping out too," Tom says with a straight, gleaming smile.

A female mark might be wont to squeal, "Euuuuhhhh, grooosssssss!"

Syd Thrip goes about it a mite differently. He pushes out all of the real toothpaste, screws back the top of the tube, and then inserts a syringe needle into the bottom of the tube. He says, "I have this syringe filled with various things at different times, depending upon the mark. I imagine your readers can create insert compounds of their own."

Pressed for details, Syd says he has refilled his marks' toothpaste tubes with library paste, hot sauce, diarrhea splashings, soap paste, etc.

Travel

Ever have someone break your mind, heart, ego, or a business deal by planning a trip, vacation, or other fun travel and then suddenly call it off? If the conversations I have with people across this country are any indication, it seems to be a common nasty that insensitive friends, lovers, spouses, associates, etc., do a lot. There are many truly nasty ways to retaliate. Rather, here is a fun one.

Announce to your mark that you've won a trip for two to Paradise Island. (You fill in a location that will make the mark flood with droolish delight.) Make all sorts of neat plans, plan big fun, and really build up the all-expenses paid nature of this trip. Really heat up the anticipation. If appropriate, heat up that angle sexually, too. The anvil is in place; now it's time to trip the hammer. There are two basic ways to drop the hammer:

1. Leave with someone else, with whom you've planned to really go all along.
2. Leave by yourself, which was the nature of the contest, real or imagined, all along.

Whichever you choose, your actual departure day should precede the mark-planned one by a day or two.

When the mark tries to contact you, have a friend, family member, or associate explain innocently that you are in (your so-called previously planned vacation spot), and then fill in with circumstance/details you provide before departure. Oh yeah, be sure to send the mark a nice postal card.

Trees

As a lover of trees, I almost didn't include this one. But, sometimes, you have to go out on a limb and oak for the best, especially ash a last measure. You have to have an ultimate nasty for a mark and this mark has to have a favorite tree — one he would easily trade off for the death of his grandchildren. See, I am a tree fan. Okay, so you have the mark who fits. You buy a can of chemical stump remover. You drill a two-inch hole halfway through the mark's pet tree, aiming downward at a 30 degree to 45 degree angle. Pour the stump remover in this hole, then plug the hole with the cutting you removed or a fabricated one if your drill dusted it. Repeat if necessary.

Turntables

Don't ask me why, but George Orr claims a major freak-out is for a mark to find a very dead horseshoe crab spinning away on the mark's turntable "the next morning." Somehow, I bet this works well in the Southwest desert, e.g., Phoenix. Katy McCutcheon says that any small, dead animal will substitute, e.g., voles, bats, or sparrows, or you can coil a small, dead snake around the unit.

That reminded me of Big Jawn Old who once experimented by flat-rolling a bit of feline roadkill with his D9 to see of the resultant object could be hardened, cut, holed, and shaped like a record. He reports success in his experiments. But, as he hadn't yet completed his pay-back as I was writing this, he asked me to withhold further details until the next writing.

Useful Addresses

Here are some potentially useful addresses you might wish to use in your pay-back efforts. In future books, I would like to expand this list, either as a resource or as a target. I would be pleased to hear from you if you have any additions or corrections.

BUREAU OF ALCOHOL, TOBACCO &
FIREARMS
Enforcement Branch
1200 Pennsylvania Avenue
Washington, DC 20004

CITIZENS COMMITTEE FOR THE RIGHT TO
KEEP AND BEAR ARMS
Liberty Park
12500 N.E. Tenth Place
Bellevue, WA 98005

DRUG ENFORCEMENT ADMINISTRATION
1405 Eye Street NW
Washington, DC 20005

FEDERAL BUREAU OF INVESTIGATION
Nine St. & Pennsylvania Avenue NW
Washington, DC 20535

FOOD AND DRUG ADMINISTRATION
5600 Fishers Lane
Rockville, MD 20852

GENERAL ACCOUNTING OFFICE
Fraud Division
441 G. Street
Washington, DC 20002

GUN WEEK
P.O. Box 488, Station C
Buffalo, NY 14209

INTERNAL REVENUE SERVICE
1111 Constitution Avenue NW
Washington, DC 20002

U.S. DEPARTMENT OF JUSTICE
Tenth Street and Constitution Avenue NW
Washington, DC 20530

U.S. DEPARTMENT OF LABOR
200 Constitution Avenue NW
Washington, DC 20002

Vending Machines

Yo, it's Ray from Kansas City, again, and this time he's got a gripe with vending machines that spill, don't pay off, or are never attended. He's tired of losing dimes and quarters and never getting a refund, so he declared his own dividend. He took a long piece of doweling with a razor blade stuck into the end and reached way up into the machine where the empty cups are stacked. He slashed the bottoms out of about ten of them before his reach gave out. This will make ten more people unhappy enough to do something, which will make ten more people unhappy, which will — eventually beget a great deal of hassle for the vending machine company.

Bill Webster from D.C. has one of the most astoundingly simple ways of dealing with certain outlaw vending machines I have yet encountered· turn them off. His plan applies to those which need electrical power to operate or to refrigerate the contents. Judge Bill adds, "If it's a machine peddling cold soda or one that has ice cream, and either of them has ripped you off without any response from the owners, geezus, it's simple. Pull the plug."

Hmmm, why didn't *you* think of that?

Windows

If you live near a nosy neighbor who loves to peek and peer at everyone else's business but his or her own, I have a new idea to screen the view. Vaseline smeared on either plastic or aluminum screens goes on quickly and easily if warm. It makes a horrible mess and also acts like a magnet for dust and bugs. It's also hard to see through. Washing it away might be impossible, and the mark would have to replace the window screens.

Another approach, which appeals to me because it is more direct and a hell of a lot easier if you're as physically lazy as I am, is to either flash or moon the nosy peeper. Right! Simply bare and grin. You may wave or jiggle, too, if you're equipped to do so.

Wrong Numbers

No, I'm not talking about that last blind date you had. This time it's for real. You've just sat down for that wonderful roast pork dinner or with that neat Single Malt Scotch after same. You look into her/ his eyes or the single eye of the boobtube. RAANNNANNNNNGGGGG. It's your telephone interrupting your life again. You answer.

"Hey, ahhh, like, ahhh, is Emilie there," dulls back a voice sounding like something growing in a crack of a mall parking lot. Your moment of shocked silence is met with a blob of "Hey, ahhh, Emilie? Is that, ahh, you?"

Your first reaction is to scream "WRONG NUMBER" and hang up.

Don't. Here's a better way. Pause another second or two, then sound as sad and distraughtly sincere as possible when you say in a slow, low voice, barely above a whisper, "Ohmigod, you don't know . . . she just died. I'm a neighbor and everyone's in shock. It's terrible. Emilie is dead (get a catch in your voice here) . . . please don't call here."

Now, you can hang up.

There was a less negative approach to wrong numbers in the hilarious film *Ruthless People* in which Danny DeVito fielded a wrong number. His cheerful patter to the obviously obnoxious caller was something like, "Gee, I'm sorry, she can't come to the phone right now. You see, my *censored* is in her mouth and she'll be tied up for awhile. I'll have her call you back when she's *all* finished." He hung up immediately after the last word in that line.

You can adapt the idea for your own use. Despite dirty looks from my fellow film critics, I laughed like hell at that sequence. I also laugh at everything Mr. DeVito says and does. He's wonderful. What a grand attitude he expresses.

Zymurgy . . . The Last Word

As Dick Smegma told his proctologist, "Well, that's about it from this end."